Published in Great Britain 2018
ABCEJ Publishing, PO Box 714, Weybridge, KT13 3HR
www.abcejpublishing.com

All proceeds from the sale of the book will go towards charitable causes.

Printed in Great Britain by Mixam UK Limited.
A catalogue record for this publication is available from the British Library
ISBN 978-1-9999336-0-9

I dedicate this book to

- Barbara, my gift from Our Lady of Lourdes
- Catherine, Lizzie and Joe, our precious children

Contents

Acknowledgements   6

Introduction   8

Illustrations   10

Pilgrimage into the heart of Jesus   12

Bernadette Soubirous   16

1st Apparition: The joy of first meeting   21

2nd Apparition: Testing the vision   25

3rd Apparition: The invitation   29

4th Apparition: Deepening friendship   33

5th Apparition: An unforgettable smile   37

6th Apparition: Facing questions   41

7th Apparition: Conversion   45

8th Apparition: Penitence, penitence, penitence   51

9th Apparition: Go and drink at the spring   55

10th Apparition: A strange sadness   59

11th Apparition: The crowds imitate Bernadette   63

12th Apparition: Halfway to paradise   67

13th Apparition: Revival   73

14th Apparition: Sacred space   77

15th Apparition: Waiting for a sign   81

16th Apparition: The Lady reveals herself   85

17th Apparition: The candle of faith   89

18th Apparition: Bernadette says farewell   93

Epilogue   96

Terminology   98

References   104

Notes   106

Acknowledgements

I was first inspired to write this book as I listened to Fr Horacio Brito, former Rector of Lourdes, giving his interpretation of the Lourdes story. Fr Horacio inspired me through his writings, CDs and talks in many different ways: with his knowledge of Lourdes, interspersed with beautifully told anecdotes, he makes the story come to life. "Lourdes is about the Gospel," he says, with Mary always pointing the way to Jesus: that is where he starts and where I join him.

Like many other writers and lovers of Lourdes, I am indebted to Fr René Laurentin, who passed away on 10 September 2017. In this book, we will hear the words spoken by Our Lady, Bernadette and other eyewitnesses. It is Laurentin who, in a lifetime of painstaking research, compiled the definitive accounts of the Lourdes story in an opus which dates back sixty years. This book is a reminder of his achievement, for which I give thanks. The historical flow, details in the sections telling the story, the eyewitness accounts and many other references are drawn directly from his work.

My companion in creating this book has been my sister-in-law and artist, Josephine Simon, who has worked with dedication to capture the story in a way that goes beyond religious icons and shows the deep relationship of love and respect between the young Bernadette and the Lady. Even if there were no words in the book, I feel that the reader could enter into the Lourdes story through these works of art. I am deeply grateful to her for this.

My final inspiration is, with heartfelt acknowledgement, St Bernadette herself. Over the course of writing this book, I have grown to love and respect this humble and hidden person. She was filled with grace, and yet never lost touch with who she was. She is an earthenware vessel, a saint for all who would say 'yes' to God's love. She gave some cautionary advice to would-be authors writing about Lourdes: "Simple writing is the best. If we try to embellish things, we spoil them." I sincerely hope that I have respected this. My aim in writing this account is to be an instrument allowing the spirit of Bernadette and the story of Lourdes to shine through the words and the illustrations.

I would also like to thank the many other people who have contributed to this book.

In my personal journeys to Lourdes, which have been a defining part of my life, the diocese of Arundel & Brighton's Lourdes pilgrimage has always lived up to its motto and been my example of "love in action". I am grateful to those no longer with us: Lady Sarah Clutton, for her thirty-seven years of service to the pilgrimage, and Cardinal Cormac Murphy O'Connor who, as bishop, made me feel so much part of the family from the very beginning. Jane Bowyer was the sick person I looked after during my first visit, and I am sure she is a saint:

being with her, my heart was melted and I grew to love Our Lady. I remember Dr Salvo Xerri, our kind and dedicated medical director – may he, and all those who have passed on, rest in peace. I have visited Lourdes with so many friends and companions over the last thirty-six years that it is hard to single any out by name. However, I particularly remember Karin Harvey, with whom I served the pilgrimage for many years; Ray Mooney, who has inspired so many young people, and three special priests and friends: Monsignor Barry Wymes, who started the Arundel & Brighton pilgrimage; Canon Seamus Hester, who was its director for twenty-three years, and Dom Stephen Ortiger who has enthused generations of pilgrims. I thank our own Bishop Richard Moth, Fr David Parmiter (spiritual director for the pilgrimage) and Deacon Mike Thoms (the current director) for keeping the flame going. Most of all, I thank the sick and disabled who are our reason for going, and who bring so much love and meaning into our lives.

I am grateful to the many people who in the Lourdes Sanctuary are dedicated to supporting pilgrims and who have always looked after our pilgrimage, notably those in the planning office. I thank Bruno Tellier and Isabelle Waksman from the bookshop, in particular, for their encouragement for this project in its early stages; and François Labadie, Director of the Accueil Notre Dame, for helping me to place this book in the broader perspective of pilgrimage to Lourdes.

For the transformation of writings and pictures into final book form, I thank Laura Brasey for her beautiful graphic design, and for doing this work with such love and care; Fr David Parmiter, Deirdre Leach, Adrienne Dines and Tom Kent for reading through the book and giving me helpful feedback; Catherine Simon for invaluable guidance on the structure of the book; Catherine Fitzsimons for her incredible copy editing and proofreading skills; and Violaine Kangou and Silvia Liberati for their first-class and thoughtful translations of the book into French and Italian ; and finally Stéphanie Algré and Nausica Rosina, my friends and colleagues from **Context**, for their quality reviews in French and Italian.

And I give thanks to all others who have held me and this book in their love and prayers; my Benedictine brothers and sisters in the Lay Community of St Benedict; my parish communities in Weybridge and in Putney; my parents, Val and Derrick, who gave me the foundations of my life, and so much else; my beautiful and loving parents-in-law, Barbara and Tom; my brothers, sisters, in-laws, nieces and nephews, and other family members for always being there – the bedrock of my life; and Barbara, Catherine, Lizzie and Joe for supporting me in this project to the end.

Introduction

"While all paths are possible, the journey we have chosen to use to uncover the value of pilgrimage is the story of Lourdes. Millions of people make the physical journey to this special place every year. It is almost impossible to describe what a pilgrimage to Lourdes is like, and it is hard to measure the impact it has on one. The best way to see it is through its fruits: many people find that their hearts are touched, they gain new perspectives and, often, find a new direction in life.

This book is for those who want to go on an inner pilgrimage, and who may go on a physical pilgrimage to Lourdes or to another holy destination at a later date."

With these words, which touch the essence of pilgrimage, Adam Simon, a lover of Lourdes, invites us to enter into the heart of Jesus.

For some, Lourdes means processions; for some, it is prayer; for others it is the Virgin Mary and Bernadette; for yet others it is the sick and the helpers or young people, and so on. It is true that Lourdes is all those things. And yet it is not only that. Above all, Lourdes is a grace, and like all grace, it overflows and adapts to all the differing circumstances of our life. It is not just any grace, it is the pre-eminent gift of the Gospel leading us to convert because the Kingdom of God is near (see Matthew 3:2).

Indeed, when Bernadette is at the Grotto contemplating the Mother of God, she tastes something of the Kingdom of God. For Mary is not a goddess: she is a human being shaped by God. Therefore, in contemplating Mary, Bernadette tastes the mystery of the Redemption brought by the gift which the Son of God, Christ, gives to all humanity. Let us never forget that Mary Immaculate is the fruit of the cross of Christ.

This is the main intuition that Adam Simon wants to share with us through his account, aided by the beautiful drawings of Josephine Simon.

A second point Adam makes is that the essential is derived from God acting through real events, the meeting between two people: the Mother of God, Our Lady of Lourdes, and Bernadette Soubirous. This meeting points to another, with Christ himself. The central core of the Lourdes message, deeply Mariological, Christological and ecclesial, is the meeting with Christ, the Saviour of the world.

The last aspect of this book to appreciate is how, through a pilgrim's perspective, the author invites us to discover the way in which we can today appropriate the experience of Bernadette. The book is like an open door to those who want to make a pilgrimage, and, therefore, takes into account the three pilgrims that each one of us carries in the deepest part of our heart:

- The first pilgrim, connected to what Pope Francis calls the gestures of popular piety: touching the rock, drinking water from the spring, lighting a candle.
- The second pilagrim, linked to the big celebrations and traditional devotions of the Church: participating in the Eucharist, praying the rosary, doing the stations of the Cross.
- The third and final pilgrim is the one open to the grace of the sanctuary itself and asks: "What can I do to change my life for the good of others and for myself?" This is the real sense of a pilgrimage and so the author invites us to the summit of this process: conversion.

In conclusion, I would like to thank Adam Simon while quoting him: *"So, now we are ready to enter into the story of Bernadette and the Lady, to be captivated by the faith and perseverance of this young girl and, with her, to make a pilgrimage into the heart of Jesus, meeting him in his words and his life."*

- **Fr Horacio Brito**
  Rector Emeritus of the Lourdes Sanctuary
  Lead Chaplain of the Hospitalité Notre Dame de Lourdes

Illustrations

1ˢᵗ Apparition   "I started to say the rosary." Bernadette

2ⁿᵈ Apparition   "The more I threw the holy water, the more she smiled." Bernadette

3ʳᵈ Apparition   "Would you kindly have the grace to come here for a fortnight?" The Lady

4ᵗʰ Apparition   "My dove, hiding in the clefts of the rock, in the coverts of the cliff, show me your face, let me hear your voice; for your voice is sweet and your face is lovely." Song of Songs

5ᵗʰ Apparition   "I live with the smile of the Virgin." Comte de Bruissard

6ᵗʰ Apparition   "My job is not to make you believe, my job is to tell you" Bernadette

7ᵗʰ Apparition   "Bernadette was no longer Bernadette; she was an angel from heaven plunged in unspeakable delights." Jean-Baptiste Estrade

8ᵗʰ Apparition   "Go on your knees and kiss the ground in penitence for sinners." The Lady

9ᵗʰ Apparition   "I found a tiny amount of water which was like mud." Bernadette

10th Apparition "She then looked sad as though she were about to cry." Antoine Clarens

11th Apparition "How I love to remember the sweet moments spent under your gaze so full of goodness and mercy for us." Bernadette

12th Apparition "Oh! How good it was there. I thought myself halfway to Paradise." Abbé Dézirat

13th Apparition "Go and tell the priests to build a chapel here and to come here in procession." The Lady

14th Apparition "She stood up with a heart full of sadness." Louise Fourcade

15th Apparition "She was prayerful, modest, reflective and immersed in her own inner world." Jeanne Védère

16th Apparition "I am the Immaculate Conception." Mary, the Mother of God

17th Apparition "We saw the flames in between her fingers." Antoinette Tardhivail

18th Apparition "Mary never looked more beautiful." Bernadette

Pilgrimage into the heart of Jesus

Digging deep

Sometimes we ask ourselves big questions: "Why am I here?", "What is life all about?", "Where am I going?" Faced with these questions, we can choose to skate along the surface of life or we can dig beneath and search for meaning. This book is for those seeking a deeper purpose in life, who feel a longing for what St Paul called "the unknown God" (Acts 17: 23). God is unknown today because formal religion is in disrepute, yet people have never lost their yearning for a view of life which goes beyond, but remains in harmony with, the material world. In today's world people hunger for purpose in their lives, in their work, and in their relationships. While the story in this book is rooted in Catholic history, it is, like all great tales, a universal narrative with themes which appeal to our humanity. It is about a young girl who faces great adversity and, in the process of overcoming it, becomes a hero in whose life we find inspiration and meaning. As Pope St John Paul put it, "There are questions which have their common source in the quest for meaning which has always compelled the human heart. In fact, the answer given to these questions decides the direction which people seek to give to their lives."[1]

A journey or a pilgrimage?

One way of setting a direction in life is by going on a journey. The young take time off to see the world, and people of all ages invest in opportunities to see beyond their own culture and narrow horizons. If this journey is about more than visiting sites but also about discovering truth, then we are pilgrims – even when we do not apply the term to ourselves. The word is heavy with religious meaning, but it also has a universal use: it signifies a journey with a special purpose. Restless, seeking truth or meaning, a pilgrim goes on a journey, leaves comfort behind and engages on a journey of discovery, often with others. On pilgrimage, people belong and, in belonging, they recognise the importance of others and feel their own sense of worth. The group knows the value of letting people travel at varying paces, with their own rhythms, picking up stragglers at any time. It is through love and caring for each other that the group bonds, and the shared values transform the journey into a pilgrimage.

Religious pilgrimage

There are many different forms of religious pilgrimage. Our world is full of incredible diversity. Every religion has pilgrimage stories which define its community. We travel in different churches or religious traditions, practise an assortment of charisms, devotions and disciplines, and take our inspiration from a variety of people. Today many people choose to undertake their inner journey through meditation or mindfulness. This method allows people to bring calm, peace and much-needed perspective to their lives. In the Christian tradition, we follow Jesus through his life and mission. With him as guide, the destination is eternal life, and, as pilgrims, we travel with others who are seeking the same goal. The objective is not to escape from the world, but to engage with it at every stage of the journey. There is also a long-established Christian tradition of pilgrimage to holy places – Rome, Vézelay, Canterbury, Santiago de Compostela, Jerusalem and, more recently, Lourdes, to name a few. Pilgrimage is not only the physical journey to a holy place, it is also the spiritual journey – engaging in an active inner search.

This pilgrimage

So, while all paths are possible, the journey we have chosen to use to uncover the value of pilgrimage is the story of Lourdes. Millions of people make the physical journey to this special place every year. It is almost impossible to describe what a pilgrimage to Lourdes is like, and it is hard to measure the impact it has on one. The best way to see it is through its fruits: many people find that their hearts are touched, they gain new perspectives and, often, find a new direction in life.

This book is for those who want to go on an inner pilgrimage, and who may go on a physical pilgrimage to Lourdes or to another holy destination at a later date.

The apparitions it describes have three phases, each with a different mood. The first seven, when the Lady first reveals herself to Bernadette, are a period of joyful discovery. Then the mood changes and the words, actions and gestures in the following five apparitions are penitential. The focus moves outwards in the last six, starting with the missionary thirteenth apparition.

Each chapter is dedicated to one of the apparitions and starts with the story of the day. This is kept as factual as possible, listing who was there and how long the apparition lasted, and leaving the reader to appreciate what happened from eyewitness accounts. The voice of Bernadette is captured wherever possible or relevant, and great prominence is given to the ten recorded statements of the Lady. In the story, we explore the exchanges between the young Bernadette and the Lady in the Grotto. We stay with them – opposite the Grotto, or walking with Bernadette and her companions to or from it. Some of Bernadette's famous encounters during the period of the apparitions get only a cursory treatment: meetings with police, prosecutors, and even the parish priest are a distraction – the purpose of the book is to help us sit in the Grotto, and to make it our home.

The vision is referred to as 'the Lady' until the last phase of the story. Bernadette listened, acted and passed on all the messages because of the beauty of the person and her words, not because of her title. Bernadette never claimed that she was encountering the Mother of God until the Lady revealed her name, during the sixteenth apparition and, from this moment, we too call her by her name. This is important for our pilgrimage: we too will experience the privilege of being invited into a full relationship with the Lady when she reveals her identity.

Following the story of each apparition, and the eyewitness accounts, there is a short reflection to try to make sense of what happened. This includes a religious or spiritual interpretation of the events of the day.

There is a picture to illustrate each day's apparition. The images show different aspects of Bernadette. We have many eyewitness descriptions of her appearance, as well as photos of her. The picture incarnates the story, and helps the reader to develop an intimacy with Bernadette. At high points, the artist has also included the Lady, trying to depict this heavenly being as Bernadette described her: a young girl, the same size and age as herself.

No pilgrimage would be complete without inviting the pilgrim to make acts of faith to support their search for truth. In the 'My Pilgrimage' section of each chapter, the reader is asked to act through prayer or service. By the end of the book, the author hopes, the reader will have had a mini experience of pilgrimage which will feed their spiritual life and give them an appetite for more.

Because the story of Lourdes is Gospel-focused, each chapter includes a short piece of scripture to bring out the parallels between the apparition and the life and teaching of Jesus. These sections are headed 'Lectio Divina'– a term used to describe a prayerful reading of the scriptures.

The book is intended to be ecumenical and accessible to people of all backgrounds: it is an open invitation to people of all traditions to get to know Bernadette, Mary and Jesus through this story. Inevitably, certain terms used are more familiar to those who practise their faith in the Catholic tradition. We have therefore included a chapter on Catholic terminology and attempt to use simple, lay language wherever possible.

So, now we are ready to enter into the story of Bernadette and the Lady, to be captivated by the faith and perseverance of this young girl and, with her, to make a pilgrimage into the heart of Jesus, meeting him in his words and his life.

Bernadette Soubirous

Between 11 February and 16 July 1858, a young girl called Bernadette Soubirous experienced eighteen apparitions of the Virgin Mary in a cave on the outskirts of Lourdes, now known as the Grotto. In the course of these encounters a miraculous thing took place – a young girl became the friend and confidante of the mother of the Lord Jesus Christ. Much of what happened in these exchanges is hidden: they took place largely in silence, very few words were recorded, and Bernadette maintained her natural reserve during and after the apparitions. And yet, over the course of the five months, we see the growth of an intimate relationship of trust, obedience and love. In this book we are going to ponder all eighteen encounters. There are no specific words recorded from some of the meetings, but we will stay with Bernadette in faith as she fulfils her promise to go to the Grotto each day, remaining with her throughout the whole journey.

Bernadette was an unlikely person to be chosen as the recipient of a divine message. The eldest of the four children of François and Louise Soubirous, she was born on 7 January 1844 and when she was baptised, the following day, the bells rang out, as was the custom for legitimate children. The first ten years of her life in the provincial town of Lourdes, were carefree and happy.

But then her family went from relative ease and comfort to abject poverty. Her father lost his job. In 1857, François was falsely accused of stealing two bags of flour and imprisoned. However, he had to be released because there was no proof to substantiate the accusations. The baker had named François as the thief because he was the poorest and most miserable person around. Bernadette became known as "the daughter of the thief, Soubirous". Her health was never strong, she was illiterate and, when the apparitions started, she had not yet made her first communion.

As St Paul says, God "chooses the weak to put shame to the mighty" (1 Corinthians 1: 27), and so Bernadette is a perfect choice in his eyes. She is an instrument of grace who listens and faithfully transmits the messages she hears. The gestures and actions of Bernadette and the Lady carry a profound Gospel message of repentance, prayer, joy and life in the Spirit, obedience to God, and a call to be missionary disciples, like Bernadette herself. She is called from humble origins, gives a prophetic message and experiences great joy but also suffers intensely in delivering this message. The story (not Bernadette) rises to glory in the miracles that ensue, the conversions, the bringing back of people to the Church and to Jesus. Our Lady is with her throughout, guiding and reassuring her, never more so than during the humiliation of the ninth apparition.

This girl was called to be the messenger of the Most High in an age in which rationalists were saying that religion was no more than superstition. She confounded everyone. As the situation developed, and more and more people were drawn to this incredible phenomenon, the remarkable strength of her character was confirmed. Let no one underestimate the faith of this child. She withstood the doubts of her family, humiliation in front of crowds, intense questioning from the police, and the bullying of the parish priest. On many occasions, she was ordered not to go back to the Grotto, but her response was simple: she had promised the Lady she would, and so she went.

So, as we follow the journey of faith of this young girl, let us open our hearts to the divine inspiration which made her into a great saint and example of faith.

The Joyful Apparitions

"I started to say the rosary." Bernadette

1st Apparition, 11 February

The joy of first meeting

Our story starts on a cold winter's day. A fourteen-year-old girl from a miserably poor family goes with her sister and friend to collect wood. She is pious and serious, always carrying her rosary with her and loved especially by her father.

Bernadette had recently come back to Lourdes after spending time in nearby Bartrès to ease her chronic asthma. She returned to the dank cell known as the Cachot, where her family lived, because she was keen to prepare for her First Holy Communion. Although it would have been better for her to stay in Bartrès, she was determined to come home.

The three girls are on an expedition to find wood for the fire. They cross the River Gave by the Pont Vieux and make their way towards the Savy Mill, where they are spotted by Antoine Nicolau, the miller. To keep warm, Bernadette wears stockings and the family's single, patched-up, white hood.

Her two companions wade across the water to go towards the Grotto of Massabielle. Bernadette tries to join them, but, afraid to cross the water in case she gets wet, she remains in safety.

For Bernadette, it is love at first sight when she beholds a heavenly presence, the sweetest, most beautiful person she has ever seen. She later described her as a "girl in white, no bigger than me"[2] and called her 'the Lady' or 'Aqueró', a patois word meaning 'that'. The lady is young, but Bernadette always avoids being too precise and later says "she did not have a specific age."[3] The eyewitness account below tells us about Bernadette's experience. The Lady graciously invites Bernadette to come forward, but Bernadette is too reserved. And, then, the vision disappears.

In the aftermath, Bernadette quizzes her sister and friend, asking them twice, "Didn't you see anything?"

"No. What did you see?" Toinette knows that something is up, and manages to extract the story from Bernadette, swearing to keep it a secret.

"My God! How I would like to go back to the banks of Massabielle," she says longingly to her sister. What she does not anticipate is the domestic storm that will ensue when Toinette lets the secret out.

Eyewitness accounts from this day

I lifted up my eyes in the direction of the Grotto. I saw a lady dressed in white: she had a white dress, a blue sash and a yellow rose on each foot, the same colour as the chain of her rosary. When I had seen that, I rubbed my eyes; I thought I was mistaken. I put my hand in my pocket; I found my rosary. I wanted to make a sign of the cross; I could not bring my hand to my forehead: it fell down. The vision made the sign of the cross. Then my hand trembled; I tried to do it and I could. I started to say the rosary; the vision moved her own beads, but she did not move her lips. When I had finished my rosary, the vision disappeared all of a sudden. I asked the two others if they had seen anything, they said no.[4]

-Bernadette, from her first account, written on 28 May 1861

She was surrounded by white light which did not dazzle me.[5]
-Bernadette to a priest in 1866

Reflection

—

Bernadette was an ordinary Bigourdane peasant girl. She had no idea of what would happen in her life. We travel on a path and then something changes us forever. We meet someone, fall in love and then our life is never the same again. Bernadette's life was transformed in the moment by the River Gave when a light-filled vision, preceded by the sound of wind bringing familiar echoes of the presence of the Holy Spirit, erupted into her life.

About this apparition

Time and duration:
13:00, 15 minutes

Number present: 3

Notable people present:
Toinette Soubirous and Jeanne Abadie

Lectio Divina

It was to shame the wise that God chose what is foolish by human reckoning, and to shame what is strong that he chose what is weak by human reckoning."

1 Corinthians 1: 27

My Pilgrimage: Awakening to the presence of God
—

The first step of pilgrimage is to open your heart and mind to the spiritual world. It is always there, but we are often too busy or wrapped up in ourselves to see it or, more importantly, to feel it. For Bernadette, the spiritual world broke into her life with a light-filled vision on this day. So, get up early and, with a fresh mind, go to a place from which you can watch the sun rise, and allow yourself to be caught up in the beauty of the dawn. This prayer exercise is a foundation for your pilgrimage: put yourself in the presence of God and open your heart to him.

Lord, as I start my pilgrimage, help me to awaken to your presence. You are there in the constancy and beauty of the dawn, but I do not see you. Help me to recognise you, and to live in the hope that you will come closer to me. With Bernadette, weak by human reckoning but chosen by God, let me look out of myself towards you, and invite you deep into my heart.

"The more I threw the holy water, the more she smiled" Bernadette

2nd Apparition, 14 February

Testing the vision

There is great concern in the Soubirous household when Bernadette recounts her experience. Her mother's reaction is fear and denial: "Poor me – your eyes have deceived you! All you saw was a white stone." Her parents forbid her returning to the Grotto, fearing that people will scorn them, a family from the poorest level of Lourdes society drawing attention to itself.

Bernadette is not put off. The following Saturday, she goes to Abbé Pomian for confession for the first time. He acknowledges that her vision could be benign and that she should not be afraid.

On Sunday, her friends, supported by François's employer Jean-Marie Cazenave, persuade her father to allow her to go back, and they run to the Grotto by a different route, through the woods. Before leaving, the cautious Bernadette stops in the parish church and fills a bottle with holy water.

Bernadette flies down the zig-zag path which leads to Massabielle and is the first to arrive. Her asthma disappears – it does not stop her running and, indeed, it never interferes with her as she prays, talks and walks in the Grotto during the apparitions. Scarcely has she completed a second decade of the rosary when she sees the vision again. For her there is nothing as important in this world as the return of this friend and her smile.

Bernadette can now put this vision to the test: this is why she has brought the holy water along.

I started throwing holy water saying to her that if she came from God she was to stay, and if not to go. She started smiling, and bowing her head. The more I threw the holy water, the more she smiled and bowed her head, and so seized with terror, I sprinkled her until the bottle ran out.[6]

The vision is cut short because one of the girls, Jeanne Abadie, throws a rock from the zig-zag path as a joke. Bernadette is shocked into a deep trance. The girls panic and fetch Antoine Nicolau, the miller, who takes her off.

Her mother is still suspicious. "Naughty girl, you are making the whole world run after you," says Louise Soubirous after collecting Bernadette from the mill.[7]

Eyewitness accounts from this day

Bernadette was on her knees, her eyes wide open, facing the niche in the rock, her hands joined, the rosary between her fingers; tears were flowing from her eyes. She was smiling and had a beautiful face, more beautiful than any I had ever seen. I was troubled and pleased to see her like this, and all day my heart was touched when I thought of her.[8]

-Antoine Nicolau

We went on the road back to the town, and I was convinced that I had said an eternal goodbye to my cave.[9]

-Bernadette

Reflection

—

Bernadette went to the Grotto concerned that she could be going to meet a bad spirit and so this was, at first, the most terrifying of the apparitions. But the benign nature of the vision soon became evident – the smile she saw when she sprinkled Aqueró with holy water was the proof she needed. From now on Bernadette could trust this person. Bernadette was so touched by the respect shown to her that, describing this second encounter later, she said, "She looked at me as a person looks at another person."

The first sign of love is the way that we look at each other. When the vision first appeared, Bernadette shouted to her friends: "There she is! She is looking at you." Her look of love covered all of them. Jesus, when faced with a rich young man who was not prepared to part with his wealth, "looked steadily at him and loved him" (Mark 10: 21). There is a famous story of St Jean Vianney, the curé d'Ars: he once met a peasant who spent hours in church in adoration of the Blessed Sacrament. When Jean asked him what he was doing, the peasant said, "I look at him and he looks at me."

About this apparition

Time and duration:
Midday, unknown duration

Number present: 12

Notable people present:
Toinette Soubirous, Jeanne Abadie, Marie Hillo, Justine Soubies, Pauline Bourdieu, Antoinette Cazalas and other friends

Lectio Divina

"

He looks on his servant in her lowliness."

Luke 1: 48

My Pilgrimage: Journeying with others

—

A pilgrimage is something to be shared. Bernadette gathered twelve of her friends to join her on this day. When people walk and travel to distant holy places, part of the experience is being with others. So, see if you can find someone to share this pilgrimage with, a prayer partner. Someone that you know who looks at you with love. Or, if this is not possible, write your thoughts and feelings in a journal.

Lord, help me to open to others, and to know that, in sharing my journey with someone, I am also getting closer to you. Sprinkle my heart with holiness, and help me look at the people around me with love, taking away all desire to judge, demean or possess them.

"Would you kindly have the grace to come here for a fortnight?" The Lady

3rd Apparition, 18 February

The invitation

In the period following the second apparition, there is unease all around, and the news spreads. Mother Ursula, the superior of the nuns in the Lourdes hospice, tells Bernadette to stop her "carnival tricks", referring to that week's Mardi Gras celebrations.

Bernadette finally gets permission to go back to the Grotto a few days later through the intervention of Madame Milhet – who employs Louise Soubirous – and her dressmaker Antoinette Peyret. They are curious about the vision and Bernadette's mother feels bound to accede to their request.

On arrival, Bernadette begins by praying ("I always started with the rosary"[10]), then goes forward, signalling to her two companions to stay behind: the Lady has beckoned her to the back of the Grotto. She sees nothing at first and is confused. Then she looks over to the right and smiles as she sees the Lady floating in a niche. This is the spot where they have their most intimate exchanges and the pattern is to continue: prayer on the outside of the Grotto, the Lady appearing in the niche, and communication in the intimacy of the cave.

The Lady speaks for the first time today, pronouncing three important phrases. Each word transforms the course of this short but intense relationship. Her words lead to Bernadette's enduring sense of commitment and purpose, which will help her weather many difficulties.

"Would you please have the kindness to write down your name?" asks Bernadette, on tiptoes, holding up a pen and paper Madame Milhet has given her.

"*It is not necessary,*" replies the Lady, laughing benevolently, and Bernadette joins her in laughter. When she hears the Lady's "sweet and gentle" voice, she knows that this is not an illusion. "*What I have to say does not need to be written down.*"

"*Would you kindly have the grace to come here each day for a fortnight?*"

Bernadette responds immediately with a promise to do so: "I said yes to her."

"*I do not promise to make you happy in this world, but in the other.*"

At this point, while Bernadette is digesting the final words spoken by the Lady, her two companions shout at her to ask the Lady her name, and Bernadette is confused. "But I asked her, in a loud voice."[11] The ladies had heard nothing and so Bernadette explains what has been said to her.

On the way home, Madame Milhet asks, "And could it be the Virgin Mary?" She is the first of many to pose this question. Bernadette remains quiet, and keeps her counsel until the Lady reveals her name. How could she know? But it gives her joy to think this could be the case.

Eyewitness account from this day

We took our rosaries and all recited a whole rosary in a low voice. Bernadette was very prayerful; her eyes were fixed on the niche. We had hardly begun our prayers when she said, "She is there."[12]

-Antoinette Peyret

Reflection

—

In many ways, this is the defining apparition. It is Bernadette's Annunciation.

The first words uttered by the Lady establish her respect for the young girl – "It is not necessary. What I have to say does not need to be written down." Bernadette is illiterate; therefore, the vision will not embarrass her by communicating in writing. Moreover, when the Lady later reveals her name, Bernadette memorises her words and repeats them to the priest. Also, there is nothing to write because the Gospel is complete in itself. These apparitions and the message of the Lady are to lead people back to the Gospel and to Jesus.[13]

The Lady formulates her invitation to Bernadette very politely, using 'vous', the formal French form of 'you' that is normally reserved for adults and important people. This is an extraordinary mark of respect which makes Bernadette feel very special: it is the first time in her life that she has been addressed using 'vous'.

On this day of invitation, Bernadette fully accepts the mission with which the Lady entrusts her, and she is faithful to her promise thenceforth. At that moment, she gives herself entirely to the Lady. It is a turning point, an eternal bonding, the transformation of a young girl into a messenger of God. When the Lady speaks of happiness, it is one of the highpoints of the apparitions. Bernadette already knows about suffering but now receives a promise of eternal happiness in the other world, God's Kingdom. Her suffering will intensify over time – through continued ill-health, then through the demands of visitors from all over the world to recount her story, and, finally, through the many humiliations that she suffers as a nun. But she will never lose the sense that her true happiness comes from the other world to which the Lady introduced her on this day.

About this apparition

Time and duration:
05:45, 20 minutes

Number present: 3

Notable people present:
Madame Milhet and Antoinette Peyret

Lectio Divina

"

Let it be done to me according to your word."

Luke 1: 38

My Pilgrimage: Praying with *lectio divina*

—

Before Jesus did anything, he spent time quietly in prayer. This morning, before going to the Grotto, Bernadette went to early morning mass in the parish church, sitting in a dark corner with Madame Milhet and Antoinette Peyret. Today, try the ancient practice of *lectio divina*, a sacred and reflective reading of the scriptures. Find a place where there is quiet. Take the time to breathe in, relax and find inner peace. Ask the Holy Spirit to guide this time of prayer. Read the scripture reflection of the day – Mary's 'yes' to God's plan when she accepted the role as mother of Jesus – quietly to yourself. Then listen to your heart and leave space, spending some minutes in silence. Think about the generous and unquestioning 'yes' of Bernadette when she agreed to come to the Grotto for two weeks despite knowing the troubles this would bring. Is God asking you something? Know how liberating it is to say 'yes' to God when he makes a request. Read the scripture of the day one more time and end with *Glory be to the Father*.

Lord, help me to open my heart in prayer. Teach me how to pray. Give me the grace to listen to God and to say 'yes' in the same way Our Lady and St Bernadette respond to the invitations they received.

"My dove, hiding in the clefts of the rock, in the coverts of the cliff, show me your face, let me hear your voice; for your voice is sweet and your face is lovely." Song of Songs 2: 14

4th Apparition, 19 February

Deepening friendship

Madame Milhet wants to take charge of the situation so she brings Bernadette back to her house for the night. But Aunt Bernarde, lynchpin of the family and Bernadette's godmother, is not going to give up control so easily, so the next morning she accompanies Bernadette and Madame Milhet to the Grotto, where they find some of Bernadette's friends already waiting.

Once again, Bernadette makes the journey in haste. "She is going to break her neck," thinks Josèphe Barinque, who joins Bernadette for the first time today, and who will be back every day for the entire fortnight. "I would rather miss my work," she says.

This apparition, and the ones which follow (fifth, sixth and seventh) reflect the joy of a girl who has found her vocation, who knows why she is where she is, and what she has to do. At this stage, there are very few people watching but, later on, the growing numbers will pose a challenge.

All the hallmarks of the early apparitions are now in place. Bernadette arrives in the cold damp of the morning carrying a special candle which has been lent to her by Aunt Lucile. She moves to her place in front of the niche, and gets on her knees. Then she starts saying her rosary and, within minutes, her face becomes deathly pale. "You would think she was made of wax," says Germaine Raval. Bernadette gesticulates, inclines her head and waves her hands.

When asked afterwards what happened, Bernadette says quite simply that the Lady smiled in silence: one looks at the other and smiles, the other looks back and smiles. Two people are in a relationship of mutual love.

Eyewitness accounts from this day

She greeted [the vision] with her hands and her head: it was a pleasure to see her, as if all her life she had learnt nothing other than how to make these greetings. I could do nothing but watch her.[14]
-Josèphe Barinque

"There is someone who sees a beautiful young girl, so beautiful that she could be the Holy Virgin or else our Elisa."[15]
-Josèphe Barinque to Emmanuélite Estrade (Elisa Latapie, a friend, had died recently)

Reflection

—

Bernadette, like Elizabeth greeting Mary at the Visitation, feels total joy at receiving a visit from the mother of her Lord. She is like the lover from the Song of Songs – she just cannot wait to see her "dove, hiding in the clefts of the rock." Above all, Bernadette wants her beautiful Lady to "show her face, and let me hear your voice." Love is communicated to Bernadette through the "sweet voice and the lovely face" of the Lady.

Through fidelity to her promise to come every day for two weeks, Bernadette is getting to know the Lady. Every minute she spends in her presence is joy. Sometimes these early apparitions are passed over because very little happens. That depends what story is being told. Here we want to meditate on the love that Our Lady poured out on a young girl.

This joy never leaves her and, when she visits the Grotto for the last time, on 3 July 1866, Bernadette, with tears in her eyes, says to her fellow nuns, "The Grotto was my heaven."

About this apparition

Time and duration:
06:00, 15 minutes

Number present: 8

Notable people present:
Madame Milhet, Aunt Bernarde, Louise Soubirous, Josèphe Barinque, Germaine Raval, Madeleine Pontic, and others

Lectio Divina

> **"**
>
> *Mary went into Zechariah's house and greeted Elizabeth … who said, 'Why should I be honoured with a visit from the mother of my Lord?'"*
>
> Luke 1: 40, 43

My Pilgrimage: Finding sacred space

—

Sacred spaces are referred to throughout the Bible – the burning bush for Moses, the cave where God passed in front of Elijah, the Temple in Jerusalem. When I step into the Grotto, I immediately know and feel that I am in a holy place. Sometimes we need to go out of our familiar surroundings in order to find God. Bernadette accepted Madame Milhet's hospitality and spent the night at her house. So, find a special place – you can create a sacred space in your home, or go to a church or a beauty spot – to continue this journey of prayer. Use this time to feel God's love for you. Just stop and be in his presence for as long as you feel comfortable. Maybe you could go away on retreat for a day – or more – to mark the start of this pilgrimage of faith.

Lord, I come into your presence with a heart full of joy, like Mary going into Elizabeth's house. I thank you for the gifts of friendship and family, for the love that has been poured into my heart. Help me to create sacred space in my busy life – time for prayer, listening and reflection. Help me to create an environment where I can grow closer to you. I pray for all people to find their vocation like Bernadette did, and I pray especially that young people may consider giving their lives to ministry, religious life or priesthood.

"I live with the smile of the Virgin." Comte de Bruissard

5th Apparition, 20 February

An unforgettable smile

The news of Bernadette's visions is spreading throughout Lourdes by word of mouth. In spite of the desire of Madame Milhet and the family to keep her visits to the Grotto private, people are drawn by accounts of the wonders witnessed. Today, the number attending grows from eight to thirty.

Bernadette sets off from Madame Milhet's house wearing a borrowed black hood. She is accompanied once again by her mother, but Aunt Bernarde, who had been emotional and fearful at the sight of her niece in ecstasy during the previous day's apparition, remains behind.

Bernadette faithfully takes her place. One of the great gifts that Bernadette has is the ability to make a deliberate and beautiful sign of the cross. Later on, when she has joined the convent, the nuns will be impressed by this and try to imitate her "…but in vain, and we would then say, 'It's clear that Our Lady taught her how to do it.'"[16]

Almost predictably, the Lady appears soon after Bernadette starts saying her rosary. As on the previous day, the apparition lasts for fifteen minutes and, when it is over, a veil of sadness comes over the young visionary's face.

Two people present for the first time, Rosaline Cazenave and Louise Lannes, comment on the beauty of Bernadette's unforgettable smile.

Some accounts say that Bernadette receives a secret prayer "for her alone" on this day or the next. Bernadette, like Our Lady, has much to ponder in her heart.

Eyewitness accounts from this day

When I got there, I thought about kneeling to say a Hail Mary … The child began her rosary with her eyes fixed on the niche, without blinking. We found it extraordinary when she ended with her wonderful bows … We left feeling quite awestruck.[17]

-Rosine Cazenave

I heard a long "y-e-s" which came from the throat or the chest, it sounded like a sigh … her face became all smiles, it was no longer the same Bernadette – the angels in heaven must be like that … Often in the night, when I wake up, I try to reawaken the picture of that face and, above all, the smiles and those lovely bows.[18]

-Louise Lannes

About this apparition

Time and duration:
06:00, 15 minutes

Number present: 30

Notable people present:
Madame Milhet, Louise Soubirous, Rosine Cazenave, Germaine Raval, Louise Lannes, Eléonore Pérard and others

---

Reflection

—

There is a touching story about Bernadette's smile. In July 1858, le Comte de Bruissard was staying nearby, at Cauterets in the Pyrenees, and he had the opportunity to meet Bernadette and speak to her.

"How did she smile, the Lady?" I asked.

The little shepherdess looked at me with astonishment, then, after a moment of silence she said, "Sir you would have to be in heaven to recreate that smile."

"Could you not do it for me? I am a doubter and I don't believe in the apparitions."

The face of the child grew dark and took on a severe expression. "So, sir, do you think I am a liar?"

I was disarmed. No, Bernadette was not a liar, and I was about to go on my knees to beg forgiveness.

Then she added, "Since you are a sinner, I am going to recreate the smile of the Virgin."

Since then I have lost my wife and two daughters, but I do not feel alone in the world. I live with the smile of the Virgin.[19]

Lectio Divina

"

Mary kept all these things, pondering them in her heart."

Luke 2: 19

My Pilgrimage: An invitation to Jesus

As we get deeper into the pilgrimage we may start to feel that we are not only journeying with friends, but also with someone else. Today at the Grotto, one of Bernadette's friends, Rosine Cazenave, said a *Hail Mary* "in case it is the Holy Virgin." In the Gospel story, two disciples were walking from Jerusalem to the village of Emmaus, when a third person came to join them. At first, they did not recognise him, and only afterwards did they realise that it was Jesus, who had risen from the dead. Afterwards they said, "Did not our hearts burn within us as he talked to us on the road and explained the scriptures to us?" (Luke 24: 31). Invite Jesus to be present with you on your journey. Start your time of prayer by doing a slow and meaningful sign of the cross, like Bernadette did before each apparition. This ancient tradition joins our belief in God as three persons – Father, Son and Holy Spirit – to the Cross where the Lord Jesus showed the depth of God's love for mankind. Then read the scripture of the day. Spend time in quiet reflection, feeling the presence of the Lord in your life and praying that he will make your heart burn as you read the scripture in his presence.

Lord, give me the gift of faith in you, a loving God in three persons. I invite you to join me on this pilgrimage of faith. Help me to ponder on the mystery of your love through the Cross of Jesus and through your Word. Give me, like Bernadette, a ready smile to light up the day of those around me.

"My job is not to make you believe, my job is to tell you." Bernadette

6th Apparition, 21 February

Facing questions

The night before, Aunt Bernarde had seized back the initiative from Madame Milhet and brought Bernadette home to the Cachot. Although she has played such an important role in supporting Bernadette, Madame Milhet now disappears from the narrative.

The Soubirous party, which, for the first time, includes Aunt Basile, are surprised to find one hundred people waiting at the Grotto, even though they had left earlier than usual in the hope of arriving before any crowds appeared.

Today Bernadette faces questions from three different institutions – the medical profession, the clergy and the police. For the rest of her life, she has to deal with constant demands to repeat and explain what happened.

The first test is from Dr Dozous, a doubter who wants to investigate Bernadette during her visionary ecstasy. He finds nothing untoward:

"I wanted first to check the circulation of her blood and her rate of breathing, so I took one of her arms and put my fingers on the radial artery. Her pulse was gentle and regular; her breathing easy. There was no sign of nervous excitement." [20]

Bernadette is not bothered by this or by any subsequent medical investigation.

The second examiner is Abbé Pène, one of the clergy of Lourdes, who asks to see Bernadette. She is tired but dutifully answers his questions. What he hears convinces him of her sincerity, and he continues to follow events closely, questioning her again on 24 and 25 February, and listening to the accounts of his sister, Jacquette, who goes to all the apparitions from 23 February onwards.

Lastly, after Vespers that evening, Bernadette is summoned by Dominique Jacomet, the police commissioner. She stands up to his bullying remarkably well and shows great aplomb when someone says they are going to put her in prison. Her response is, "I am not worried – if they put me in there, they will take me out." [21] It may be this evening that Bernadette makes one of the most famous statements attributed to her (the exact time when she said it is not clear): "My job is not to make you believe, my job is to tell you."

The only real sadness of this day is that her father agrees to forbid her from going back to the Grotto. Bernadette cries but says nothing to her father – she is an obedient girl.

Eyewitness account from this day

Bernadette moved into the Grotto as soon as I let go of her arm. I noticed that her face, which up to now had expressed the most perfect joy, grew sad, and two tears rolled down her cheeks … her pulse was gentle and regular. [22]

-Dr Dozous

Reflection
—

Bernadette was remarkably clear and consistent in her articulation of the messages she received, and never felt browbeaten by any questioning of her story, even though people were aggressive and sometimes even rude. Maybe the Lady had already prepared her for this. On this day, she certainly embodied the Gospel: "When you are handed over, do not worry about how to speak or what to say; what you are to say will be given to you when the time comes, because it is not you who will be speaking; the Spirit of your Father will be speaking in you" (Matthew 10: 19–20).

Following her example, the Lourdes Sanctuary today embraces scientific investigation. It is the only pilgrimage centre in the world to have a medical bureau, which was founded in 1883 and reviews the cases of all those who claim miraculous healing. Since 1858 only sixty-nine cures have been recognised as miraculous. These sit at the intersection of reason and faith: only once the physicians agree that there is no known medical explanation for the cure, are the religious authorities able to pronounce whether it is, in their view, miraculous.

About this apparition

Time and duration:
06:00, 15 minutes

Number present: 100

Notable people present:
Louise Soubirous, Aunt Basile, Aunt Bernarde, Dr Dozous, Pierre Callet, Martin Tarbès and others

Lectio Divina

"

Do not be afraid, Mary, for you have found favour with God."

Luke 1: 30

My Pilgrimage: Praying with the rosary

—

Today, join with Bernadette in saying the prayer of the rosary. Meditate on the five Joyful mysteries – the Annunciation, the Visitation, the Incarnation, the Presentation of Jesus in the Temple, and the Finding of Jesus in the Temple. As you say this ancient prayer, bring your life's challenges, whatever they are – relationships, work-related, financial, health – to the Lord. He cares about every detail of your life.

Lord, I offer my life with all its challenges to your loving care. I entrust myself to you. Help me, like Mary, to overcome fear and to trust in you always.

"Bernadette was no longer Bernadette; she was an angel from heaven
plunged in unspeakable delights." Jean-Baptiste Estrade

7ʰ Apparition, 23 February

Conversion

Today the story focuses on a man – Jean-Baptiste Estrade – who became a great witness to the apparitions, wrote three accounts of what happened, and who travelled the length and breadth of France telling the story of his conversion.

After the fourth apparition, Josèphe Barinque spoke enthusiastically to her friend Emmanuélite Estrade, saying that she would not be surprised if Bernadette were seeing the Holy Virgin. Emmanuélite remained indifferent, though she did mention it to her brother, Jean-Baptiste. Two days later, after the sixth apparition, Josèphe saw her again and said, "Yes, yes, it is true – the little one sees the Holy Virgin." This time Emmanuélite was impressed and woke up her brother to pass on the news. The next day, although he was sceptical, he went to see Abbé Peyramale, the parish priest, to seek his authorisation to go and check out what was happening. Permission was granted immediately. "Go there! People are speaking about this and I would not be cross for a serious person like yourself to go and see what is happening," said Peyramale.[23]

Early on 23 February, following one of the two days of the fortnight when there was no apparition, he and Emmanuélite went to the Grotto. They were positioned next to the visionary.

"She took out her rosary and started praying. Soon her face seemed to reflect an unknown light: she started staring, her face radiant, full of wonder, delight and happiness as she looked at the opening in the rock. As I witnessed the transfiguration of this child, all my previous opposition melted away, giving way to an extraordinary feeling which took over, despite myself. I had the certainty, the irresistible intuition that a mysterious being was present … Bernadette was no longer Bernadette; she was an angel from heaven plunged in unspeakable delights … she was afraid, it seemed, to drop her eyelids for one instant lest she lose the enrapturing sight of the marvel she was contemplating."[24]

His life was changed forever by what he saw. In what has become a definitive account of the apparitions, published in 1889, he wrote that his hair had now turned grey, said he did not dare think about his iniquities, and asked that, when he appeared before her son, Mary would remember that she had seen him at the Grotto.

Eyewitness accounts from this day

I have seen Rachel [a very famous actress] in Toulouse and Bordeaux, she is magnificent, but infinitely below Bernadette. No, my dear Abbé, no, Bernadette is not acting: she is in the presence of a supernatural being.[25]

-Estrade to his neighbour Abbé Pène

Kind sirs, when a street entertainer shows in the main square a sheep with two tails or two heads, you all run there. Well, I have seen better than that. This child in her ecstasy is a picture which no painter could equal. Explain it as you wish …[26]

- Estrade to the men of Lourdes gathered in the Café Français, in response to their jokes, laughter, and taunts

I came incredulous, I left a believer.[27]

-Estrade

About this apparition

Time and duration:
06:00, 1 hour

Number present: 100

Notable people present:
Aunt Bernarde, Jean-Baptiste Estrade, Emmanuélite Estrade, Jean-Brice Dufo, Eléonore Pérard, Fanny Nicolau, Joseph de la Fitte, Romain Mengelatte and others

Reflection

—

As this joyful period of discovery comes to a close, we can imagine Bernadette giving a shout of joy like that which forms the opening of the Magnificat. Nothing in this, the longest apparition to date, could distract her from her discourse with the Lady. Even when Eléonore Pérard, who found out about Bernadette's vision when she overheard her speaking to Abbé Pomian in the confessional, plunges a needle into Bernadette's shoulder, she does not flinch.

Lectio Divina

*My soul magnifies the Lord;
my Spirit rejoices in God
my Saviour."*

Luke 1: 46

My Pilgrimage: Praying with Adoration
—

As we continue our pilgrimage, so we move further out of our comfort zone. Today Jean-Baptiste Estrade decided he would accompany his sister to witness events at the Grotto even though he was cynical. So, today, think about extending your personal prayer. It may help to go into a church, find the spot where the Blessed Sacrament is reserved and spend time in adoration.

Lord, help me to turn towards you and to experience conversion. Take away my heart of stone and give me a heart of flesh. Let all my being praise and magnify your name. I pray for the courage of Jean-Baptiste Estrade, as I seek to deepen my understanding of the truth.

The Penitential Apparitions

"Go on your knees and kiss the ground in penitence for sinners." The Lady

8ᵗʰ Apparition, 24 February

Penitence, penitence, penitence

Today, as Bernadette enters into the vision, she goes deathly pale. "My God, she is going to die!" a woman in the crowd cries out. Jean-Brice Dufo, a lawyer, cannot look – he feels as though he is not entitled to, almost as if he is stealing something. Fanny Nicolau bursts into tears, as do others. Remember, at this stage, most of the crowd of three hundred and fifty people have come to see the spectacle of a sweet fourteen-year-old girl in a visionary trance. They have no idea that they are going to see a profound expression of sorrow and abasement.

There is a lot of movement inside and outside the Grotto. At several points, Bernadette comes out of her state of ecstasy. She is upset because people are touching and disturbing a wild rose, and this makes the Lady disappear. To the crowd, she seems to be talking. Bernadette thinks that others can hear her but today she learns that the conversations she has with the Lady are for her alone, and that no one else can catch them. There is a growing intimacy in their relationship.

Later she explains. The Lady says: *"Penitence. Pray to God for the conversion of sinners. Go on your knees and kiss the ground in penitence for sinners."* And then she graciously adds: *"Would it bother you to do that, Bernadette?"*

Bernadette accedes to the Lady's request, open-hearted and without questioning, just as she had agreed to her invitation to come to the Grotto each day for a fortnight. She gets on her knees and kisses the muddy ground of the cave the locals call 'the sty' because of the pigs that shelter there. She discovers the meaning of penitence not through catechesis, but through seeing how sad the Lady's face is when she talks about sinners. Bernadette's face, alternating between joy and sorrow, reflects what she hears and sees. For the rest of her life, she will never stop finding occasions to pray for the conversion of sinners.

By the end of the day, Bernadette has conquered at least one other person. On the way back, Dominiquette Cazenave, who, that morning, had criticised what she thought were Bernadette's scornful looks, says to someone, "No, she is not inventing things."[28] Bernadette is winning the hearts of the people of Lourdes one by one, though she will put these people to the test the very next day.

Eyewitness accounts from this day

Fanny Nicolau asked Bernadette if the Lady spoke to her.

"Goodness! You were so close. Didn't you hear anything?" asked Bernadette.

"How does she talk to you? In French or in patois?" asked Fanny.

"Oh, come on! Why would she speak to me in French? She talks in patois and she says 'vous'."[29]

Reflection

—

Today the mood changes as we move into the penitential phase of the apparitions. It is markedly different. With Bernadette and the eyewitnesses, we are entering a deeply testing time, of questioning, facing up to life's realities, experiencing sorrow and being challenged to change. The witnesses, growing in number every day, are deeply moved and pass through a variety of emotions: pity, disgust and, for some, conversion. In this phase, the penitential gestures of Bernadette take on a profoundly evangelical meaning. Bernadette humbles herself at the request of the Lady. She feels an acute sense of sin, reflecting the sadness of the Lady when she asks her to pray for sinners. Maybe we too can enter this phase on our knees with Bernadette who is leading us deeper into faith. If we were able to see the sadness on the Lady's face, would our hearts be converted too?

About this apparition

Time and duration:
06:00, 15 minutes

Number present: 350

Notable people present:
Aunt Lucile, Dominiquette Cazenave, Fanny Nicolau, Dufo family, Jacquette Pène (sister of Abbé Pène), Mlle Peyrade, Emmanuélite Estrade, Sr Marie de l'Assomption Fourcade and others

Lectio Divina

"

The time is fulfilled and the kingdom of God is at hand; repent, and believe in the gospel."

Mark 1: 15

My Pilgrimage: Acknowledging my weakness
—

One of the first steps in holiness and conversion is to know that we are sinners and to believe in the love of God which overcomes all sin. I do not have to go on my knees or kiss the ground like Bernadette, but simply recognise the reality of sin in my life. Sin is when I put myself before other people or God. It is the desire to possess things or people. It is when I hurt others. Sin can poison our lives, destroy relationships and be addictive. St Paul says, "I cannot understand my own behaviour. I fail to carry out the things I want to do, and I find myself doing the very things I hate" (Romans 7: 15). Consider speaking to a priest or minister or your pilgrimage companion to let go of the things that weigh you down. It is important to talk or, if this is not possible, to write in a journal: in this way, you address those parts of your life which block you from greater openness to God. Doing this will give you a sense of unburdening and relief, and open your pilgrimage into a new level of meaning.

Lord, I come to you as a sinner with a sorrowful heart, knowing that I fall short of what and who I am called to be. I go on my knees with Bernadette to ask you to show me your merciful and abundant love, and to lift me up by removing my burden of sin.

"I found a tiny amount of water which was like mud." Bernadette

9ᵗʰ Apparition, 25 February

Go and drink at the spring

This is the central apparition and, during it, the miraculous spring appears. At two o'clock in the morning, in spite of the rain, people start to gather. When Bernadette arrives at half past five, the Grotto is full. Although the groundwork had been laid the day before, people cannot bear the sight of Bernadette on her knees. They can hear her murmuring, "penitence, penitence, penitence."

Bernadette wanders in and out of the Grotto, towards the River Gave and then back again. Her face is sad and perplexed; she is irritated. Eventually, she climbs up the slope in the interior of the Grotto on her knees. She scrabbles in the dirt, making balls of mud, and having done this four times, she cups dirty water in the palm of her hand and drinks it. She rubs the mud on her face and, to cap it all, she grabs a handful of a wild salad leaf that has a bitter taste and eats it. Her aunt Bernarde is so revolted by her antics that she gives her niece a hard slap – but not before wiping the mud from her face.

Most people leave disgusted or feeling pity for the girl, although some sense that something special is happening. For example, Marie Portau leaves with a great desire to return, and Madeleine Courrade weeps at the humble gentleness of Bernadette.

Later, Bernadette explains that the Lady spoke of water, and that she had wandered back and forth because she could not work out which water the Lady was referring to. The Lady had also asked Bernadette for a second time to pray for the conversion of sinners.

Once again Bernadette demonstrates her complete trust in the Lady and people drink the water that has appeared. Jean Domingieux is the first, before Bernadette even leaves the Grotto. Jeanne Montat fills the first bottle of water from the spring, and says to her father, "You must drink this water."

Eyewitness accounts from this day

Aqueró said, "Go and drink at the spring and wash yourself in it."
Unable to see any, I went to drink from the Gave. But she made a sign
with her finger for me to go under the rock. I went there and found
water which was like mud.
"Why did she ask you that?"
She didn't say. She also said "Go and eat of the grass which is there."[30]
-Bernadette

People were laughing at us. We left quickly to escape the crowd: some
people followed us as if it was a comedy.[31]
-Aunt Bernarde

I am bewildered and no longer understand anything.[32]
-Jean-Baptiste Estrade

About this apparition

Time and duration:
05:30, 1 hour

Number present: 350

Notable people present:
Marie Portau, Louisette de Tiné, Jeanne-Marie Carrère were the first present, arriving at 02:00. Pauline Cazaux & her brother came at 03:30. Catherine Oustallet, Jean Domengieux, Jean-Baptiste Estrade, Aunts Basile, Lucile and Bernarde, Dr Dozous, Martin Tarbès, Elfrida Lacrampe and others were also there.

Reflection
—

In these three central days of the eighth, ninth and tenth apparitions,
Bernadette is living the Gospel. She is re-enacting the humility of God made
man and is like the suffering servant who prefigures the Passion of Jesus:
"a man of sorrows and familiar with suffering, a man to make people screen
their faces; he was despised and we took no account of him" (Isaiah 53: 3).
Humility comes from the Latin humus meaning 'earth', and here is Bernadette
rubbing her face in it. When Jesus assumed human form he "did not cling
to his equality with God, but emptied himself to assume the condition of a
slave, and became as men are" (Philippians 2: 6–7). Bernadette is in the mud
with us, and she is, like Jewish people at Passover, eating the bitter herb of
suffering. Of course, we are revolted by this. We hate seeing suffering and
humiliation and do everything to stop it happening – rightly so. But it is part
of the human condition, and Bernadette, like Jesus, is most powerful when
she is simply in the dirt with us. And then ...

And then, the marvel.

From this human tragedy, life-giving water comes forth in a miraculous
spring, just as water flowed from the side of Jesus crucified when he was
pierced with a lance. The water of Lourdes, which started flowing today,
is a sign of the outpouring of God's love and grace in the midst of our
sinfulness and suffering. It is a powerful symbol of the new life, renewal
and grace poured out for each one of us. In the water of baptism, we die
and are reborn with Christ.

Lectio Divina

"

One of the soldiers pierced his side with a lance; and immediately there came out blood and water."

John 19: 34

My Pilgrimage: Entering into the Paschal mystery

—

Today, as pilgrims with Bernadette, we go into the heart of Jesus. We learn the truth about Jesus's life, death and resurrection. Take time to go to a church and find the holy water at the entrance. Bless yourself with the water. As you do so, offer the humiliation and suffering in your life to God, and ask him to transform it into new life. He will be sure to answer this heartfelt prayer.

Lord, give me the courage to believe in you whatever the circumstances. Give me trust in you that, like Bernadette's, is unshakeable even if I suffer humiliation and do not understand where you are leading me.

"She then looked sad as though she were about to cry." Antoine Clarens

10th Apparition, 27 February

A strange sadness

The day before this tenth apparition, 26 February, was the second in the fortnight when the Lady did not appear. Bernadette was inconsolable. "What did I do to her?" she asked.

But Bernadette does not lose hope and comes back again today at seven o'clock. Despite the disgust people had felt on the previous occasion, the crowd has grown to eight hundred people. All the talk in the town is of the water of the spring now flowing in the Grotto.

"There were ten or twelve people per square metre. It's true that I could only see people's heads, but I suppose their bodies were there too," wrote Antoine Clarens[33], the headmaster of a school in Lourdes, who is here for the first time today.

The prayerfulness surrounding Bernadette is palpable. "As soon as she gets on her knees, there is a general silence, a recollection which is pleasant for the soul."[34] She directs her eyes up to the niche, kisses the ground, drinks the water from the spring and, once again, when she turns around, her face is muddy and her smile is "strange and unbearable"[35] rather than touching, as it had been during the earlier visions. Clarens has to turn his eyes away.

Today, for the third time, the Lady asks Bernadette to pray for the conversion of sinners, and repeats "Penitence, penitence, penitence."

Clarens leaves feeling unsure, but decides to write a journal of his experiences which he will later send as an official report to the Prefect of the Hautes-Pyrénées, Baron Massy. The following day, he goes to the Cachot and speaks to Bernadette. He is taken by her charm, and the clarity of her responses. "The Vision ordered me to do acts of penitence; for myself first of all, and then for others."[36] Clarens does not exclude the possibility of a miracle, but he prefers to be prudent and ends his report with a very Lourdes-like conclusion: "Let Science tell us if the girl is having hallucinations, and the religious authorities pronounce if there has been a miracle. Until these two authorities give their verdict – and they will – we should take as our watchword: *wait and doubt*." He calls his report *The Mysterious Grotto of Lourdes or the Apparition of 1858 with its character up to this day* and he will wait until the fortnight is up to submit it.

Eyewitness account from this day

She fixed her eyes on the opening which holds the tangle of brambles and for a few moments she prayed, with a candle in her hand. Then she grew pale and smiled and bowed in greeting. She then looked sad as though she were about to cry, but soon smiled again and then bowed once more. That strange sadness which spread over her face for an instant, her smile which defies all description, her strange pallor, the position of her eyes, made her unrecognisable. You would have said she no longer belonged to this world.[37]

-Antoine Clarens

Reflection

—

Following the eighth and ninth apparitions, Bernadette continues to express her deeply felt penitence through repeated gestures and the sadness of her appearance. While no one other than Bernadette sees the face of the Lady, it is clear that her own face is a pure mirror of what she sees: a Lady of Sorrows who invites us to meditate on our sinfulness and our need for redemption. "When the Lady is happy, I am happy. When she is sad, I am sad," says Bernadette.

About this apparition

Time and duration:
07:00, 15 minutes

Number present: 800

Notable people present:
Aunts Bernarde and Lucile,
Antoine Clarens
and others

Lectio Divina

Whoever drinks this water will get thirsty again; but anyone who drinks the water that I shall give will never be thirsty again: the water that I give will turn into a spring inside him, welling up to eternal life."

John 4: 13–14

My Pilgrimage:
Praying with the Stations of the Cross
—

Today I continue in a spirit of penitence, as the Lady asks. I reflect on the words that Jesus spoke to the Samaritan woman at the well. He talks of a spring welling up inside me offering eternal life. What does this mean? How do I tap into that spring? One way of getting closer to Jesus is to accompany him on his final steps through the traditional penitential devotion of the Stations of the Cross. We walk with Jesus, we fall with him, we meet his mother and the others he encountered, we go to Calvary, and we hear his final words of love and total forgiveness from the Cross. "Never was love, dear King; never was grief like thine!"[38]

Lord, I recognise my need for spiritual food and drink. With the Samaritan woman, I say "Give me some of that water, so that I may never get thirsty." Let me journey with Jesus to Calvary and know in my heart that he really loves me and is the Saviour of the world.

"How I love to remember the sweet moments spent under your gaze
so full of goodness and mercy for us!" Bernadette

11th Apparition, 28 February

The crowds imitate Bernadette

I t is a grey and rainy day. People bring umbrellas, but others protest so strongly that they have to lower them and everyone is left standing stoically in the rain. Many a modern-day pilgrim who has attended rainy Grotto masses can identify with the experience.

In the early apparitions, the people witnessing the events at the Grotto were a mixture of curious bystanders and spectators. Most were the ordinary people of Lourdes, with local notables such as Jean-Baptiste Estrade, Dr Dozous and Jean-Brice Dufo being the exception. Certain people had been moved or even converted by what they saw, but, until now, they had been individuals. Today that changes.

The crowd grows to over a thousand for the first time, and the penitential theme continues. Bernadette starts with a sign of the cross and says the rosary. For a fourth time, the Lady asks her to pray for the conversion of sinners. Bernadette gets on her knees, humbly obeying the Lady. Suddenly, there is a voice from the crowd. It is Sergeant Callet calling out to people to get on their knees. For the first time, the people in the crowds follow the gestures of Bernadette, and appropriate for themselves the message of penitence. The entire crowd kneels, prays and says the rosary while the expression on Bernadette's face alternates between one of deep joy and one of deep suffering.

Eyewitness account from this day

Bernadette listens for a few minutes with great attention … going onto her knees, she walks to the foot of the rock, kissing the ground at each step. My sister was on the path that Bernadette was following and said, "Today there is something new."

"Yes, this is new," called out the old constable. "This is getting stronger and stronger." Then he turned to the crowd and cried in a loud voice, "Kiss the ground, all of you." The crowd obeyed him immediately and kissed the ground, like Bernadette, following her as she did it. [39]

- The Abbé Pène memo

About this apparition

Time and duration:
07:00, 15 minutes

Number present: 1,150

Notable people present:
There is some speculation as to who was there, but the crowd included Jean Domingieux, Victoire Bonnecarrère, Antoinette Garros, Jeanne-Marie Garros Pierre Callet and Marie Pailhès.

Reflection

—

The apparitions are about to initiate a mass revival of popular religion in France and, aided by the railways, throughout Europe. Against a background of an Enlightenment hostile to organised religion, confidence in the simple messages of pilgrimage, penance, prayer, hope and healing could flourish, and has done so to our day. But this has also been possible because Lourdes immediately embraced science as a partner. In this light, it is not a coincidence that one year after the miracle of Lourdes, Charles Darwin published *On the Origin of Species* describing the wonder of evolution. The miracle of faith and the marvels of science go hand-in-hand or, as Pope St John Paul II put it, "Faith and reason are like two wings on which the human spirit rises to the contemplation of truth."[40]

The young girl in peasant costume and clogs, and the beautiful lady in a white dress and blue sash with roses at her feet are joined through one shared object – the rosary, symbolising their focus on the life and death of Jesus Christ. Lourdes is, above all, about the Gospel leading people into a deeper faith.

The touching soul of this young girl, poor in spirit and rich in love, has sparked a revolution of the heart. She recalled the joy of her friendship with the Lady in a prayer she wrote just before going into the convent in Nevers:

How happy my heart was good mother when I had the happiness to contemplate you! How I love to remember those sweet moments passed under your gaze, full of goodness and mercy for us!

Yes, tender mother, you humbled yourself coming to earth to appear to a feeble child and communicate certain things despite her great unworthiness. What a great example of humility. You, the Queen of Heaven and of earth wanted to use the weakest in the earth's eyes.[41]

Lectio Divina

Seeing the crowds, he went up the hill. There he sat down and was joined by the disciples. Then he began to speak. This is what he taught them: 'How happy are the poor in spirit; theirs is the kingdom of heaven. Happy the gentle; they shall have the earth for their heritage.'"

Matthew 5: 1–4

My Pilgrimage: Coming together

—

This is my pilgrimage but, in reality, I cannot journey without the help of others. Today people started an act of collective worship at the Grotto. In the modern world, many people say "I don't need to go to church, I can speak to God in my heart." That is right, we can. But we also need food and water for our journey, and we can receive that – together with all the other benefits of being with other people and belonging to a community – through the Word of God, the sacraments, collective worship and fellowship. Consider how you can link up with other people on your life's pilgrimage. If you are not already part of a church community, you may want to try joining one. Do not give up if, for any reason, the first one you try does not work. Try another. You may want to join a prayer or fellowship group in your parish. Or explore the spirituality of great saints such as St Francis, St Benedict or St Ignatius – all of whom have followers who come together in community to deepen their faith. Or there are new communities of which Taizé, the Emmanuel Community, the Beatitudes, Chemin Neuf, Focolare, L'Arche, the Neocatechumenate are examples. Many of these communities are ecumenical and welcome people of all denominations.

Lord, teach me through the example of Bernadette to be poor in spirit, gentle in heart and to live the Gospel message of the Beatitudes. Teach me to value community and the benefits that being with other people on my life's pilgrimage can bring me.

"Oh! How good it was there. I thought myself halfway to Paradise." Abbé Dézirat

12th Apparition, 1 March

Halfway to paradise

Today, for the last apparition of the penitential cycle, the numbers go up again: there are now 1,450 people. Bernadette manages to get through the crowds with the help of two soldiers who escort her to her place, and guard and protect her. Today is the only day when a priest is present – Fr Antoine Dézirat has come, against the orders of Abbé Peyramale. The crowds make way for him because he is wearing a cassock, and, as he is shortsighted, the soldiers allow him to get to within a metre of Bernadette in order to see her face close up.

Bernadette begins with a sign of the cross, starts praying the rosary, and continues with the penitential gestures including drinking of the water now flowing freely from the spring. According to one eyewitness, Jean Vergez, she drank "without taking the water in her hand"[42] from the spring, which, starting as a muddy trickle, now produces twenty-seven thousand litres of water per day.

Fr Antoine marvels at what he sees but is also very conscious of the order for priests not to be there so, despite all the efforts people have made to give him such a good view, he leaves after ten minutes. When he gets back to the seminary to tell people about the day's events, he is laughed at – one of the loudest laughs is from Fr Sempé who, ten years later, became the first superior of the chaplains of Lourdes!

On this day, the first Lourdes miracle recognised by the Church takes place. At three in the morning, Catherine Latapie, who has a withered arm, has an inner calling to go to the water to seek healing. She is nine months pregnant and walks the seven kilometres with two of her children. Somehow, she manages to plunge her arm into the muddy water and, as soon as she takes it out, she feels a great softness come over her. She finds her fingers are now supple. She joins them together in prayer, something she had not been able to do for many years. A miracle. Then she feels labour pains come on and she prays, "Holy Virgin, who has just healed me, let me get back home!" She gives birth fifteen minutes after arriving home.

Eyewitness accounts from this day

Her smile was beyond all description. The most skilful artist, the most consummate actor could never reproduce its charm and grace … What struck me was the joy and the sadness on her face. When one of these phenomena was followed by another, it happened in a flash … Bernadette alone saw the apparition, but everyone felt her presence … Respect, silence, prayer reigned all round … Oh! How good it was there. I thought myself halfway to Paradise.[43]

-Fr Antoine Dézirat

For the small number of people who have common sense, reason and science, Bernadette has a well-known mental disease: she is having hallucinations; but there is a large and growing number, on the other hand, from every social class, who believe that she is in direct communication with the Divinity.[44]

-Dutour, the Imperial Prosecutor

Reflection

—

While it is edifying and uplifting to learn about a miracle, that of today or any of the sixty-nine officially recognised cures, the real miracle of Lourdes is the faith that it has inspired in so many people. One of the marks of that faith is the vulnerability that is plainly visible on Bernadette's face when she is sad: two eyewitnesses (Dufo and Clarens) specifically said that they had to avert their eyes from Bernadette because it was too painful or difficult to look at her, and there were many others who did the same. Many wept at the sight of her. Lourdes exposes raw emotions and vulnerability, in particular through the presence of the sick and disabled who, by their example, help us to recognise our own weakness and need of healing. But this happens in the presence of a loving mother who cares for us. Mary invites Bernadette, and all of us, to be vulnerable but know that we are loved, and, in this certainty, turn towards goodness and life.

Lectio Divina

He said to the man with the withered hand, 'Get up and come forward! ... Stretch out your hand.' And he stretched it out, and his hand was restored."

Mark 3: 3, 5

My Pilgrimage: Praying with apps

—

Today I will make a list of all those people and situations which I want to bring before the love of God in prayer. Jesus says "Ask and it shall be given unto you." One day I will find out who prayed for me when I was in need of support. There are a number of electronic aids to help one be faithful in daily prayer. One is called *Universalis*, and it contains the daily prayer of the Catholic Church (the Divine Office) and readings from the mass of the day. Another is *Pray as you go* which provides a daily reflection on the Gospel. Both have websites and apps for phones or tablets.

Lord, I bring the people I love and the situations I am concerned about to you in prayer. Like the man with the withered hand, I come to you believing in your loving kindness and ask you to take away any anxiety which I feel.

The Missionary Apparitions

"Go and tell the priests to build a chapel here and to come here in procession." The Lady

13th Apparition, 2 March

Revival

We move now into the final stage of the apparitions. Bernadette no longer does the penitential practices. Mysteriously, the mood changes. This is the missionary phase.

The crowds continue to grow – 1,500 are on the Grotto side of the River Gave, most of them with no view at all of what is happening, and there are 150 on the Prairie de la Ribère opposite. Bernadette goes into the intimate space of the Grotto, and the people watching sense that something special is happening. There is evidently a conversation taking place, and Bernadette is pressed to say what was said. Before rushing off to see the priest and pass on the messages, she tells them that the Lady has asked for people to come in procession. This encourages more devotion and expectation of a miracle, as well as heightened speculation about what will happen on the final day.

The exact words of the Lady are: *"Go and tell the priests to build a chapel here and to come here in procession."*

Much has been written about the conversations which take place between Bernadette and Abbé Peyramale following this request. He is dismissive, and terrifying to talk to, but Bernadette is not put off and, by the end of the day, she is delighted and says, "I am very happy. I have done my task."[45] But the Abbé remains sceptical and refuses to do anything until he knows the Lady's name.

Eyewitness account from this day

Today ... the visionary was in a state of ecstasy for several minutes at the entrance of the Grotto, and when she came out, someone asked her what the Virgin said to her, and this is her response: "The Virgin asked for a procession next Thursday, 4 March; I will ask the priests for this to happen."[46]
-Police Commissioner Dominique Jacomet

Reflection

—

Today the Lady gives Bernadette a truly remarkable commission and, even now, after 160 years, we have barely captured the powerful impact of this request. The building of a church and the institution of a procession in Lourdes was, in fact, the rebuilding of the universal Church and mass pilgrimage in France and in Europe. Bernadette overcame the criticism of those who would have liked to dismiss the whole phenomenon as the invention of an hysterical young girl. Her poverty, simplicity and transparency, linked with her ability to articulate the detail of events clearly and consistently, meant Bernadette never let down the Lady and her mission of revival of the Church.

There are similarities in the story of the call of St Francis of Assisi. In 1205, he was in the church of St Damiano when he heard the voice of Jesus on the cross say to him, "Go, Francis, and repair my church, which, as you can see, is in ruins." He thought that Jesus was referring to the physical building; only later did it become apparent that he was referring to the entire Church. Bernadette's impact also goes way beyond the provincial town of Lourdes. As Bernadette follows today's message and turns outwards, so she is following the great commission given by Jesus before he ascended to the Father: she creates a missionary movement and a gift for the whole world.

About this apparition

Time and duration:
07:00, 15 minutes

Number present: 1,650

Notable people present:
Aunts Bernarde and Basile and many others

Lectio Divina

Go, therefore, make disciples of all the nations; baptise them in the name of the Father, and of the Son, and of the Holy Spirit, and teach them to observe all the commands I gave you."

Matthew 28: 19–20

My Pilgrimage: Reaching out to others

—

With Bernadette, I start to look outwards. How can I share my gifts with others? There are many simple things that I can do to bring the light of Christ to others. A very Lourdes-inspired activity would be to go and visit a sick or a housebound person, or invite them to a service of anointing of the sick. Many Catholic parishes have a Society of St Vincent de Paul which visits people in need in the parish, and other churches have similar outreach groups. It is not so easy to visit prisoners – you have to be trained and apply to do such work – but some people choose that as their mission. You could go to a night shelter or a foodbank, or get involved in a charity helping refugees. There will be many other forms of support you can give in and through your church. People who help others always seem to say the same thing: "I am sure I am getting more out of this than the people I am supposed to be helping."

Lord, I am an ordinary person and feel inadequate, unable to go out to others. Like Jeremiah, I say, "Look, I do not know how to speak: I am a child." And yet, you ask me to tend for the sick, to visit prisoners, to feed the hungry. So I ask you for the grace to act on your Word, and to transmit it to others through both my own words and the witness of my life.

"She stood up with a heart full of sadness." Louise Fourcade

14ᵗʰ Apparition, 3 March

Sacred space

By the time Bernadette goes to the Grotto with her mother at seven o'clock, there are a record number of people there. Her candle is in pieces by the time she arrives. She starts by saying the rosary although she can barely see the niche and has no room to make her normal gestures. Françoise Junca has come from Ossen to see the transformation of Bernadette which she has heard so much about, but nothing happens. Bernadette is visibly sad because the Lady does not appear. She cries as she leaves the Grotto, as does her mother.

This non-appearance of the Lady is, in fact, an important moment and convinces people of Bernadette's genuineness. No one who saw her sad face could doubt that she was really expecting to see someone, and was bitterly disappointed when that person did not turn up. It is a turning point for Jean-Marie Cazenave who says: "If the little one was inventing things, she would have said that she saw her today just like on the other days."[47]

But all is not lost. Bernadette goes back after lunch at the suggestion of her mother's cousin, André Sajous, and the Lady is there, smiling. This is the only time that the Lady is actually waiting for her when she arrives at the Grotto. Bernadette asks the Lady for her name but she does not get a response.

In the evening, her cousin Jeanne Védère comes to stay in the Cachot after attending a funeral. Bernadette confides in Jeanne and discusses the day's events. She tells Jeanne that the Lady was upset saying "some people came along who wanted to see what your face looked like in my presence, and they were unworthy. They spent the night in the Grotto and profaned it."[48] The holy space had been defiled.

Everyone is expectant, waiting for the big day: the last day of the fortnight.

Eyewitness accounts from this day

Father left for the Grotto at three o'clock on Wednesday morning, and, as he was leaving, he said to me, "Today, I am going to see the child in ecstasy. There won't be lots of people today because everyone will wait for tomorrow as it is a market day and, even more importantly, the final day." … On his return, he could not contain his astonishment, because he had not been able to see anything as the crowds were so great. He assured me that there were more than six thousand people.[49]

-Adélaïde Monlauer in a letter to her cousin

Yesterday, when three thousand people at least had gone to this spot, the vision did not appear for the young girl, for the first time, which seemed to affect her very deeply. It is important to make this point, which goes against the suggestion that this was a hallucination. During the day, the child came back to the Grotto, where she still found a lot of people present. The vision showed herself, but for a shorter time than on the other days.[50]

-The report made by Antoine Clarens

The next day when I arrived at the Grotto, after having said the rosary, I asked her name on behalf of the priest, but she only smiled … so he told me that she was making fun of me and I would do well not to return. But I could not stop myself from going. I went there for two weeks and I asked her each time who she was – which always made her smile.[51]

-Bernadette in an unpublished note dated 1866

About this apparition

Time and duration:
07:00, waiting ten minutes with no appearance, and then later (time unknown) for a very short apparition which lasted ten minutes

Number present: 3,500 in the morning, and 100 later on

Notable people present:
In the morning: Monsieur Monlauer, Louise Soubirous and many others.

André Sajous, her cousin, accompanied Bernadette for the second visit.

Reflection

—

We sometimes forget that Jesus and his mother were fully human and felt the emotions we feel. Nowhere is this portrayed more strongly than when Jesus is angry and expels the moneychangers from another sacred space, the Temple in Jerusalem.

All of the Lady's major appearances take place on the same weekday. The first apparition was a Thursday; a week later, the Lady invited Bernadette to come for a fortnight; the ninth apparition, when the stream was uncovered, was a week after that; and the last day of the fortnight, tomorrow, is again a Thursday. We will see that the vital sixteenth apparition also takes place on a Thursday. There are no strong associations with Thursday in the Christian tradition other than its significance as the day of commemoration of the Last Supper. Perhaps the reason is secular – market day in Lourdes was Thursday, and the Lady was thinking about how she could get her message to the maximum number of people. She has a truly missionary outlook.

Lectio Divina

> "
> *Then he went into the Temple and began driving out those who were selling; 'According to Scripture' he said, 'my house will be a house of prayer. But you have turned it into a robbers' den.'"*
>
> Matthew 28: 19–20

My Pilgrimage: Being an agent of reconciliation

—

Today we see the sadness of Bernadette and her mother as they leave the Grotto which was profaned the day before. And yet, in the afternoon, the Lady is there waiting for Bernadette and smiling in anticipation of seeing her again. Relationships break in so many families and between so many friends – small hurts build up until, one day, things get out of control and the sacredness of love is profaned. As Christians, we are called to be agents of reconciliation. Jesus said, "Blessed are the peacemakers." (Matthew 5: 9). While we may not have the professional skills needed to counsel people, we can always show love and do everything to bring healing into broken relationships. So, today, think and pray about how you can help people you know who are in need of reconciliation.

Lord, once again, I am no expert. I do not know how to mend broken relationships. Please give me the grace to reach out in love to those whose lives are in need of healing, and to be an agent of peace, as Jesus asked me to be. Help me to develop the right attitudes and to find words which will contribute to an increase in understanding and love, and help others overcome past hurts.

"She was prayerful, modest, reflective and immersed in her own inner world." Jeanne Védère

15th Apparition, 4 March

Waiting for a sign

The big day arrives. It is the end of the fortnight. The police have put special arrangements in place to keep the crowds orderly. Place Marcadal, where the Thursday market always takes place, is deserted – there are photos from the day which show that there was not a soul there. Mayor Anselme Lacadé, goes up to the chateau to watch the scene unfold and realises that Lourdes is about to be transformed. As the sun rises, he beholds an amazing sight – seven or eight thousand people are waiting patiently, spread out on both sides of the River Gave. At a quarter past seven, a little later than usual, "the visionary arrived surrounded by three or four uncles, two aunts and her father marching at the head and asking the crowd to make way for his daughter."[52]. She is separated from her cousin, Jeanne Védère, whom she had promised could be with her. Bernadette calls for Jeanne, and she is brought along. Bernadette makes the sign of the cross and starts praying the rosary. The apparition takes place in an atmosphere of prayer and expectation and lasts fifty-two minutes. This is longer than usual and timed very precisely by Jacomet. He counts thirty-four smiles and twenty-four greetings and notes them in his book.

The mayor sends a report to the prefect. Bernadette spends thirty minutes in prayer, then goes into the Grotto where "she smiles for two minutes, and looks serious for three minutes."[53]. She makes three greetings, returns to her normal station on her knees, spends two minutes looking at the niche, appearing slightly vexed, then blows out the candle and leaves with her family.

The priest has not organised a procession, despite the request of the Lady, but an amazing thing happens – a huge crowd of people processes from the Grotto to the Cachot because they want to see and be with Bernadette.

People had decided that there would be a sign on the last day of the fortnight, and they are disappointed that nothing has happened. The critics of Bernadette have a field day. The press is full of jubilant articles consigning the Lourdes apparitions to oblivion. Here is what two local papers have to say:

*Bernadette again! You will say to us; dear reader, please be patient with us as we are going to give you some details which we hope will be the last. Bernadette had announced that the pretty Lady would express her desires on the last day. What disappointment! How the poor credulous people have been humiliated! (*Le Lavedan*, 4 March 1858).*

Here is where we are and we would not be here if the parents of the so-called saint of eleven years old [their mistake] *had followed the advice of doctors and sent the sick girl to a hospital … it does not appear that what has happened at Lourdes has been judged worthy by the clergy of any serious attention. (*L'Ere Impériale* 4 March 1858).*

But God's timing is not our timing and, according to Jean-Baptiste Estrade, many people in Lourdes felt that the Lady had not yet spoken her last words.

Eyewitness accounts from this day

All souls were caught in profound contemplation, men took their hats off very respectfully, women fell to their knees, everyone felt transported at this supreme moment.[54]
-Jean-Baptiste Estrade

You were so close to the Lady; if you had just stretched out your hand a little, you would have touched her.[55]
-Bernadette to Jeanne Védère

Reflection
—

Today I learn more about God's ways. Maybe I, like the eight thousand people at the Grotto today, am here because I want something. I am looking for a sign. And then, nothing happens and I am disappointed. The sign is there in the daily transformation of Bernadette, the appearance of the spring, and, most importantly, in what we call the *kerygma* – the life, death and resurrection of Jesus Christ. I do not need anything else.

Lectio Divina

> " *I am the resurrection. If anyone believes in me, even though he dies he will live, and whoever lives and believes in me will never die. Do you believe this?"*

John 11: 26

My Pilgrimage: Being a missionary disciple
—

I am called into a personal relationship with Jesus Christ, who loves me as a unique person. I am made in his image, and he wants me to go out and tell others. Here is what Pope Francis has to say on being a missionary disciple:

> In virtue of their baptism, all the members of the People of God have become missionary disciples (cf. Matthew 28: 19). All the baptised, whatever their position in the Church or their level of instruction in the faith, are agents of evangelisation, and it would be insufficient to envisage a plan of evangelisation to be carried out by professionals while the rest of the faithful would simply be passive recipients. Anyone who has truly experienced God's saving love does not need much time or lengthy training to go out and proclaim that love. Every Christian is a missionary to the extent that he or she has encountered the love of God in Christ Jesus. So, what are we waiting for? (*Evangelii Gaudium* 120).

Lord, I am a lukewarm disciple and I cling onto many unnecessary things to help me in my journey. Teach me to have a deep personal relationship with the risen Christ, recognising his love and passion for me. Help me to be a missionary disciple proclaiming him through the example of my life, and in my words.

"I am the Immaculate Conception." Mary, the Mother of God

16th Apparition, 25 March

The Lady reveals herself

For three weeks, Bernadette quietly waits. Early in the morning of the feast of the Annunciation, moved by an inner calling and a feeling of joy, she goes to the Grotto with her Aunt Lucile. Some people are waiting there, hoping that this special day might bring another vision.

Bernadette says the rosary, the Lady joins her, and then, after their time of shared prayer, she is invited to go inside the Grotto, to the location of their most intimate exchanges. Bernadette has prepared herself for this moment, knowing that she has to find out the Lady's name for Abbé Peyramale. She stands under the niche and asks four times, "Madam, would you please have the goodness to tell me your name?" Each time the Lady smiles. On the fourth, her face grows serious and she passes the rosary into her right hand. She stretches out her arms towards the earth "with such a simple gesture a majesty shines forth."[56] Then she joins her hands at the level of her chest, lifts her eyes to the sky and says, *"I am the Immaculate Conception."* Bernadette is overwhelmed with joy, gratitude and a new sense of hope. She now knows the Lady's name and can go to see Abbé Peyramale. She has not heard this expression before, as she later testifies to the Commission of Enquiry. Indeed, Abbé Pomian will note that she has no idea of many common terms used in Christian doctrine, let alone this more obscure phrase. One thing is sure – now Bernadette has revealed this name, it will be recognised across the world.

Bernadette leaves her candle between some rocks in the Grotto, as a sign of gratitude, and so lights up the message of the Immaculate Conception. As she goes, she whispers the words of the Lady to Ursule Nicolau. Ursule passes it on to Eugénie Raval (under a seal of secrecy), who passes it on to her sister Germaine, who tells it to Dominiquette Cazenave (again under an oath of secrecy).

Meanwhile, Bernadette herself rushes to the priest's house full of joy. She bursts in. 'I am the Immaculate Conception.' Aqueró said, 'I am the Immaculate Conception.'" Peyramale is confused by this title and asks her if she is sure. Bernadette replies yes and says that, in order not to forget the words, she repeated them to herself all the way to his house. Abbé

Peyramale feels shaky and full of emotion. Quite overcome, he quietly dismisses her. "Go home now, Bernadette," he says. Left alone, he is moved to tears and knows now that it is indeed the Blessed Virgin who has appeared.

Later, Bernadette was often asked to repeat what the Lady said at this special moment. "I have never seen anything as beautiful as when I asked her how the Holy Virgin was when she said 'I am the Immaculate Conception' wrote Joseph Fabisch, sculptor of the statue of Our Lady in the niche of the Grotto, in 1863. The same was repeated by nuns who gave their testimonies during Bernadette's beatification process. On 8 July 1866, just after she had entered the convent in Nevers, Bernadette was asked to tell the nuns the story of the apparitions for the first and only time. Sister Stanislas Paschal, one of the three hundred nuns present, wrote that when she described the gesture of the Lady, it caused "unspeakable emotion".

> **About this apparition**
>
> **Time and duration:**
> 05:00, 1 hour
>
> **Number present:** 20
>
> **Notable people present:**
> Aunt Lucile, Julie Garros, Ursule Nicolau, Jeanne-Marie Tourré, Mlle Dufo, Dominiquette Cazenave and others

Eyewitness account from this day

On 25 March, the day of the Annunciation, I went to the Grotto and stood next to the visionary. It was the same setting, the spirit of God brought her to life, and I went away with the same impression. Bernadette got up this day, saying that the Lady of the apparitions, had declared that she was Mary, the Immaculate Conception.[57]

-Jean-Baptiste Estrade

Reflection

—

Today the Lady reveals herself as Our Lady. After all the quiet smiles each time Bernadette had asked her name before, she finally says who she is. She is the conception of grace. She is the conceiver of grace. She is the immaculate one, and she calls each one of us to be spotless like her, through loving her son Jesus. On this glorious day when the Lady reveals her name, and it is now clear to everyone that it is indeed the Mother of God who has appeared, she also reveals our destiny: to be holy and immaculate.

Lectio Divina

> "
> *Before the world was made,*
> *he chose us, chose us in Christ*
> *to be holy and immaculate,*
> *and to live through love in*
> *his presence."*
>
> Ephesians 1: 4

My Pilgrimage: Going out strengthened by the Eucharist

—

On this day we thank God. There is no better way to give thanks than through participating in the Eucharist, "the source and summit of our faith."[58] The final dismissal of the mass tells us to "go in the peace of Christ", and, fortified by the body and blood of Jesus, we can go out to be Christ in the world. So, today, go to a church where you can be strengthened by the Eucharist.

Lord, I come to you on this day of revelation. I particularly thank God for the gift of Our Lady, so close us to us, always leading us back to her son with a mother's love. Help me always to be thankful, and to go out to others in the peace of Christ. Help me to "be happy at all times; pray constantly; and for all things give thanks to God." (1 Thessalonians 5: 16–18). May I stay close to Jesus through listening to his Word and frequently participating in the Eucharist.

"We saw the flames in between her fingers." Antoinette Tardhivail

17th Apparition, 7 April

The candle of faith

There is a beautiful symmetry to the apparitions in Lourdes. In the beginning, there are two standalone apparitions. Then there is the central series which starts with the invitation to Bernadette to come for the next two weeks. Now we enter the closing period which also comprises two standalone apparitions – the seventeenth and the eighteenth. Rumours that Bernadette is going back to the Grotto start on 6 April when she is seen going to her confessor in the parish church. In order to avoid the crowds, and the rising level of excitement, she accepts an invitation to stay with some friends in the village of Adé. But she leaves at four in the morning in her horse and cart, and arrives at the Grotto an hour later.

She begins with a deliberate sign of the cross, and starts praying the rosary: today she will say the entire rosary, all three sets of mysteries. Dr Dozous pushes his way to the front of the crowd to stand next to her, saying that he does not come as an enemy, but as a scientific observer. As she starts the second decade, Bernadette's face is transfigured and she enters a time of ecstasy. Dr Dozous watches closely. Bernadette remains on her knees, and puts her hands round the candle, moving them up to protect the flame from the draught. The flame licks her fingers for ten minutes, but the doctor examines her and there is no sign of burns. This 'miracle of the candle' convinces Dr Dozous, who was completely cynical about the apparitions up to this point. He will say to Bernadette the next day. "I did not believe, but now I have faith: I am happy that I came to the Grotto."[59]

Inspector Jacomet writes the exact words of Dr Dozous – acknowledging that a miracle has taken place – in his notebook. The doctor becomes as loud and opinionated in his support for Bernadette as he had been in opposing and doubting her. Once again, Lourdes sees faith and science join in a strong and complementary alliance.

In the meantime, the relationship between Bernadette and Our Lady can move onto a new level, now Bernadette knows who she is. During this apparition, Bernadette goes into the Grotto to speak intimately with Our Lady who reminds her she wants a chapel to be built as soon as possible.

Eyewitness account from this day

Then she goes up a gentle slope to arrive in the Grotto, holding a candle in her hand. This is where you see her greeting the Holy Virgin, it is the only place where she speaks to her, but nobody hears anything. Sometimes you see the child's lips moving, she follows all the movements of the Holy Virgin.[60]

-Antoinette Tardhivail

Reflection

—

Candles are an almost universal symbol of faith, and there is no shrine where they have played, and still play, such a significant role as they do in Lourdes. Today, row upon row of candles burn in front of the Grotto, reflecting the prayers of countless pilgrims who light them saying, "This candle continues my prayer." It is a beautiful and moving sight. Antoinette Peyret brought a candle to the third apparition, and Bernadette carried candles, lent by Aunt Lucile, on each subsequent visit. After the sixteenth apparition, she left a candle behind as a symbol of faith. Today the candle symbolises not only her faith but also her love of God – she is close to the heart of Jesus and holds the light of Christ in her hands. We do the same when we light a candle in an act of faith. As the saying goes, lighting a candle is better than cursing the darkness.

Today Bernadette kindles a spark of love, and the flame is going to spread. We are sad now, as we know that the apparitions are coming to an end. But we are also filled with enormous joy, as Bernadette passes on the mission to others who will keep the flame burning. Bernadette is starting to think about what she will do with her life: not an easy choice for a living saint surrounded by fame. But her dream is to enter religious life and this is what she will eventually do, entering the Convent of St Gildard in Nevers in July 1866.

About this apparition

Time and duration:
05:00, 1 hour

Number present: 200–300 at the start, 1,000 by the end.

Notable people present: Bernadette kneels between Germaine Raval on her right and Justine Cassou on her left. Antoinette Tardhivail and her two sisters Marie and Théotiste, Dr Dozous and Martin Tarbès are among others present.

Lectio Divina

> **"**
>
> *When Jesus spoke to the people again, he said: 'I am the light of the world; anyone who follows me will not be walking in the dark, but will have the light of life.'"*
>
> John 8: 12

My Pilgrimage: Developing a Rule of Life
—

After this intense period of pilgrimage we too, like Bernadette, may want to find a way to integrate these experiences into our life. One way of allowing the light of Christ to enter is to establish a rule of life: we can decide which of the different elements of the pilgrimage we want to practise on a daily or regular basis, changing our one-off pilgrimage into a sustained journey of faith. Different forms of prayer, sacramental life, belonging in community, outreach to others – each of these elements from the rich tapestry of pilgrimage can form part of a rule of life.

Lord, wherever I am on my faith journey, I thank you for bringing me to this point. Help me to live in a way in which faith and spiritual values have a place. Let me make a home for Our Lady like St John did, and welcome Jesus her son into my life.

"Mary never looked more beautiful." Bernadette

18th Apparition, 16 July

Bernadette says farewell

O n 4 June 1858, between the seventeenth and eighteenth apparitions, Bernadette receives her First Holy Communion. When asked whether communion or the apparitions were more special, she replies, "The two things go together, but cannot be compared. I was very happy in both."[61]

It is now time for Bernadette to grow smaller and for the miracle of Lourdes to grow bigger, with hundreds of thousands of people coming in pilgrimage, obeying the commands of Our Lady.

But she does say goodbye to the Holy Virgin. On the feast of Our Lady of Mount Carmel, she feels the Virgin calling her.

It is evening (this is the only apparition that takes place at this time of day). The Grotto is boarded up by order of the prefect. To avoid the crowds, she goes with Aunt Lucile by a different route, one which takes her onto the meadow on the other side of the river from the Grotto. Bernadette is disguised and hidden. They light a candle. Bernadette is pale and in ecstasy. She kneels and says the rosary.

This is the last time Bernadette sees Our Lady on this earth.

Bernadette's words describing Mary's beauty on the day of the last apparition remind us of Our Lady's moment of crowning glory, her coronation in heaven, described in the Revelation of St John: "A great sign appeared in heaven: a woman clothed with the sun, with the moon under her feet and a crown of twelve stars on her head" (Revelation 12: 1).

While there is sadness in this final apparition, Bernadette's life in the other world of grace and sanctity, that promised to her by Our Lady in the third apparition, is now firmly established.

Eyewitness account from this day

"Mary never looked more beautiful," says Bernadette after the apparition. "But how were you able to see at such a distance, and with the barrier?" "I saw neither the planks of wood, nor the River Gave. It was as if I was in the Grotto, at the same distance as the other times. I only saw the Holy Virgin." [62]

-Bernadette

Reflection

—

Through Bernadette, we were offered a new moment of salvation – on her 'yes' hung the whole divine plan to bring renewal to the Church. She brings a gift to the Church in the same way as St John the Apostle did. From the Cross, Jesus gave Our Lady to St John, telling him to "make a place in his home for her." Because of the apparitions in Lourdes, Our Lady is honoured throughout the world – there are churches dedicated to Our Lady of Lourdes in every corner of the globe. There are Grottoes in the most unlikely of places, as well as the one in the Vatican Gardens that was inaugurated in 1905 by Pope St Pius X. Bernadette came back to Lourdes at the end of January 1858 to make her first communion. A few months later, prepared for her communion day by her personal catechist – Our Lady – Bernadette opens her heart to Jesus in a very special way, and that is where she leads us now. We too are invited to open our hearts.

About this apparition

Time and duration: 20:00, 10 minutes

Number present: 4

Notable people present: Aunt Lucile, Françoise Brinjot and one other who saw her were invited to come along. They watched from the Prairie across the river from the Grotto.

Lectio Divina

Seeing the disciple he loved standing near her, Jesus said to his mother, 'Woman, this is your son.' Then to the disciple he said, 'This is your mother.' And from that moment the disciple made a place for her in his home."

John 19: 26–27

My Pilgrimage: Celebration!

—

Today I reach the end of this pilgrimage with Bernadette and the start of a new journey. So it is time to celebrate. Our faith is based in the joy of the resurrection, in the Lord Jesus whose first miracle, working closely with his mother, was to turn water into wine at a wedding feast. "Do whatever he tells you," Mary said, as she encouraged him to help the wedding hosts who had no more to give. And the wine he produced was vintage: "You have kept the best wine till now," said the guests (John 2: 5, 10).

So, in order to celebrate the end of this Lourdes pilgrimage, why not invite some friends over to your home? Have you ever had your house or flat blessed? If not, you could invite a priest or minister to do so. The important thing is to celebrate, and talk about the good things which the Lord and his blessed mother have done for you. If you enjoyed getting to know Bernadette and the other characters in the story of Lourdes, you could always use this occasion to start planning a physical pilgrimage there: you will love the journey, the experience of prayer at the Grotto and the healing that the Lord brings. But that is another story.

Lord, I celebrate the joy of your resurrection. I celebrate the life that you have given me. I celebrate your mother Mary, and your servant Bernadette who, through her humility, opened the door to heaven for so many people. I ask your help to live a life of prayer and closeness to you. Help me to be an instrument of joy, hope and reconciliation to those around me.

Epilogue

The setting up of a Commission

On 28 July 1858, less than a month after the final apparition, Bishop Laurence of Tarbes, set up an investigation into what had happened during the events at the Grotto. He said the purpose was to "shed light on the religion and piety of thousands of believers, respond to a public need, fix uncertainties and calm everyone." He established a commission which called witnesses to testify in the parish church in Lourdes. Bernadette appeared on 17 November and once again told everyone what happened, with the same simplicity and lucidity, never embellishing the facts. The commission met witnesses, officials, and Bernadette's family and friends. They interviewed all those who claimed they had been healed, and, after rigorous examination, named those whom they believed had been miraculously cured. On 7 December 1860, Bernadette again appeared before Bishop Laurence and the twelve members of the commission. When she re-enacted the sixteenth apparition, an observer saw two tears rolling down the bishop's cheek and, after the meeting, he said to a vicar general "Did you see that child?"[63]

The criteria

When he had digested the evidence, Bishop Laurence commented on three elements of the situation and this constituted the basis of his opinion.

• First, the character of Bernadette herself. She showed no signs of hysteria, was always reliable and consistent in her statements, and, therefore, he stated that the girl "truly heard and saw a being who called herself the Immaculate Conception."

• Second, the attitude of the crowd who flooded there for the apparitions, and showed great recollection and prayer despite the very cramped conditions. He noted that, since the apparitions stopped, people had continued to come in large numbers to pray there. "They prove, by their attitude of prayer, that they feel a divine spirit bringing life to this rock which has now become so famous."

- Third, the healings and impact on people who came to the shrine. "People who were already Christians have come to strengthen their faith; people who were frozen in indifference have been brought back to practising the faith; obstinate sinners have reconciled themselves to God after calling on Our Lady of Lourdes to look on them with favour." Scientists examined the water in detail, and concluded that it was pure and common H^2O. "What power has produced the healings? These healings are the work of God."

The decree

Bishop Laurence waited a year from the closing of the commission before publishing his final decree on 18 January 1862. During that time, he made progress towards buying the land around the Grotto in order to be able to build a church there, and start constructing what has become the Lourdes Sanctuary. The decree itself is a moving declaration of faith in what happened.

> *We judge that Immaculate Mary, Mother of God, truly appeared to Bernadette Soubirous on 11 February 1858 and on the days that followed, to the number of eighteen times, in the Grotto of Massabielle, near the town of Lourdes; that this apparition displays all the characteristics of truth, and that the faithful and are justified in believing that it is certain.*

The bishop also authorised the cult of worship of Our Lady of Lourdes, and committed to building a church in the area of the Grotto, in accordance with Our Lady's request.

Never, in the history of the Church, has there been an official decree so soon after a series of supernatural happenings that so clearly states the faithful can trust in the authenticity of the events.

Terminology

Devotions

The Blessed Sacrament In Catholic tradition, the real presence of Jesus in the consecrated host, known as the Blessed Sacrament, is a treasure of the faith. One of the first things that a Catholic will do when entering a church is to locate the tabernacle where the Blessed Sacrament has been reserved and will pay particular respect to that area of the church. Traditionally when people walk up to the tabernacle, they will go on one knee in a practice known as 'genuflection'. Every day in Lourdes there is a procession in which the Blessed Sacrament is carried aloft under a canopy (reminding us of Old Testament practice with the Ark of the Covenant) and transported to the underground basilica, where a service of blessing (Benediction) takes place. The high point of this service is when the chief celebrant blesses the sick and disabled pilgrims with the Blessed Sacrament. Many of the officially recognised Lourdes miracles have taken place at the moment of this solemn blessing.

Adoration of the Blessed Sacrament A common practice, which builds on this devotion, is to pass time in prayer in front of the Blessed Sacrament. This is a time when people can adore the special gift of the Lord in his real presence. Some churches, such as the basilica of Sacré-Coeur in Paris, maintain perpetual adoration – this means that, except when services are taking place, there are always people praying in front of the Blessed Sacrament, which is exposed above the main altar. In Sacré-Coeur, this practice has been unbroken for one hundred and thirty years. If this interests you, then you can easily sign up to spend the night there by going to http://www. sacre-coeur-montmartre.com/english/. Or you can visit Tyburn Convent in London, which is run by the same order of nuns as in Sacré-Coeur, and also does perpetual adoration https://www. tyburnconvent.org.uk/. In Lourdes, there is a chapel in which the consecrated host is exposed for the practice of adoration and, during the service of the Blessed Sacrament procession, there is always a prolonged time of silence to allow all pilgrims to spend time in contemplation and adoration.

The Rosary There are 150 psalms, and it has long been the practice of religious, priests and some laypeople to recite the entire psalter on a four-weekly, two-weekly or weekly cycle. In the Middle Ages, those who were not literate would have had difficulty doing this. Therefore, a simpler devotion was created to allow common people to contemplate the life and mysteries of Christ, in the company of his mother Mary.

How to say the rosary
Traditionally, there were three sets of mysteries – the Joyful, Sorrowful and Glorious – each of which reflects a different stage of Christ's life from the annunciation of his birth to his death and resurrection. Each mystery is divided into five decades, and each decade has ten *Hail Marys*. This meant that when someone said a full rosary they recited this prayer 150 times, so matching the number of psalms in the psalter. In 2004, Pope St John Paul II added another set of mysteries – the Luminous – covering the time of Jesus' earthly ministry from his baptism to the institution of the Eucharist. The rosary was the foundation of all the exchanges between Bernadette and Mary, and now, in Lourdes, there is a nightly torchlit

procession in which one of the sets of mysteries is recited prayerfully by thousands of pilgrims walking from the Grotto to the esplanade in front of the main basilica.

Rosary prayers

Start with the *Apostles' Creed*

I believe in God, the Father Almighty, Creator of heaven and earth; and in Jesus Christ, his only son, our Lord:
who was conceived by the Holy Spirit, born of the Virgin Mary; suffered under Pontius Pilate, was crucified, died and was buried. He descended into hell. The third day he rose again from the dead. He ascended into heaven, is seated at the right hand of God the Father Almighty; from thence He shall come to judge the living and the dead.
I believe in the Holy Spirit, the Holy Catholic Church, the communion of saints, the forgiveness of sins, the resurrection of the body, and life everlasting. Amen.

Then say one *Our Father*

Our Father
who art in heaven
hallowed be thy name;
thy kingdom come,
thy will be done,
on earth as it is in heaven.
Give us this day our daily bread,
and forgive us our trespasses,
as we forgive those who trespass against us;
and lead us not into temptation,
but deliver us from evil. Amen.

Hail Mary three times:

Hail Mary full of grace,
The Lord is with you.
Blessed are you among women,
and blessed is the fruit of your womb, Jesus.
Holy Mary, Mother of God,
pray for us sinners,
now and at the hour of our death.

And say one *Glory be to the Father*

Glory be to the Father, and to the Son, and to the Holy Spirit.
As it was in the beginning, is now and ever shall be, world without end, Amen.

Each decade of the rosary is made up of one *Our Father*, ten *Hail Marys* and one *Glory be*

Conclude with *Hail, Holy Queen*, and a closing prayer.

Hail, Holy Queen, mother of mercy; hail, our life, our sweetness and our hope. To thee do we cry, poor banished children of Eve: to thee do we send up our sighs, mourning and weeping in this vale of tears. Turn then, most gracious advocate, thine eyes of mercy towards us and, after this our exile, show unto us the blessed fruit of thy womb, Jesus, O clement, O loving, O sweet Virgin Mary! Amen.

Let us pray. O God, whose only begotten son, by His life, death, and resurrection, has purchased for us the rewards of eternal life, grant, we beseech thee, that meditating upon these mysteries of the Most Holy Rosary of the Blessed Virgin Mary, we may imitate what they contain and obtain what they promise, through the same Christ Our Lord. Amen.

Stations of the Cross One third of the text of the Gospels is dedicated to a narrative about the death and resurrection of Jesus. Sometimes, it is hard to take in the magnitude of the self-giving love of Jesus. The devotion of the fourteen Stations of the Cross emerged in the early Middle Ages as a way of meditating on Jesus's sacrifice, allowing people to follow him from his condemnation to death, through his walk to Calvary and crucifixion, to the moment his body was laid in the tomb. A fifteenth station – the Resurrection – was later added to remind people of the end of Jesus's journey. Most pilgrims to Lourdes will spend some time meditating on the Stations of the Cross. As well as the beautiful stained glass pictures depicting the stations inside the underground basilica, which are helpful for meditation, there are three different places where people can practise this devotion in the open air. The High Stations go up the mountain of the Espélugues; the Riverside Stations are on a calm meadow by the waters of the River Gave, opposite the Grotto; and the new Marble Stations, further along that same meadow, contain stunning modern sculptures.

The Sign of the Cross The practice of making the sign of the cross dates back to earliest Christian times, and is to be found in Catholic, Orthodox and some reformed churches. It is a prayer and a blessing that opens up the believer, promoting a state of readiness to worship God. St John Vianney said that a genuinely made sign of the cross "makes all hell tremble." Bernadette always started her prayer before each apparition with a sign of the cross, and, as she died, it was the last thing that she did before entering into eternal life.

Holy water In every church there is a stoop of water which has been blessed by the priest. People use this holy water to bless themselves as they come into the building. The water is blessed when it is used in the font for baptism, or at Easter, when people renew their baptismal vows. It may be used for house blessings, and in other prayer services. In Lourdes, the water that flows from the miraculous spring is considered holy without an additional blessing.

Spiritual life

First Holy Communion The Eucharist holds a place of pre-eminence in the Catholic Church and, traditionally, children receive their First Holy Communion a young age, after a period of instruction. This is nearly always at a separate time to the sacrament of Confirmation. In Bernadette's day, young people undertook this rite of passage at the age of twelve. Bernadette was two years' late, which explains her impatience to leave Bartrès and come back to Lourdes to prepare for the special day when she would first receive the body of Christ.

Sacraments of Healing Sacraments are an earthly sign of a heavenly reality. There are two sacraments of healing.

The first is the **Sacrament of Reconciliation**. This sacrament, formerly known as confession, reveals God's loving forgiveness, which is like that of the father in the story of the prodigal son. God is the only person who can forgive sins, but Jesus gave his apostles the power to forgive or retain sins on his behalf. When a person goes to receive reconciliation, they are washed clean from sin. Bernadette begins her time with Our Lady by making her very first confession. In Lourdes, the sacrament of reconciliation is deeply embedded in the spirituality of the shrine. On numerous occasions, Our Lady asked Bernadette to pray for the conversion of sinners, and going to the sacrament of reconciliation is a powerful witness that conversion is taking place and sin is being rejected. It is also a step towards healing: very often it is sin which makes us unwell – we may be angry, bitter, selfish and, when we speak about how we feel and what we have done, we let go of a massive burden.

The second is the **Anointing of the Sick**, in which God's desire to heal us is made manifest. When a sick person approaches Jesus to heal him, and asks him if he wants to do it, Jesus replies immediately, "Of course I want to heal you," (Matthew 8: 2). In the old days this sacrament was reserved for people who were about to die. In recent times, this has become a celebration of God's healing love. In his letter, St James enjoined the first disciples to practice this sacrament:

Any one of you who is ill should send for the elders of the church, and they must anoint the sick person with oil in the name of the Lord and pray over him. The prayer of faith will save the sick person and the Lord will raise him up again; and if he has committed any sins, he will be forgiven. So, confess your sins to one another, and pray for one another to be cured; the heartfelt prayer of someone upright works very powerfully (James 5: 14–16).

In Lourdes, the high point of many pilgrimages is the celebration of this sacrament. As the helpers carry in the oils which are used to anoint the sick, there is a palpable sense of Christ coming to heal his people. On no other occasion is there a greater sense of shared prayer.

Lectio divina Lectio divina is a prayerful reading of the scriptures. Reformed churches have traditionally encouraged a personal reading of the scriptures, but it is something lay Catholics have recently rediscovered. In the decree *Dei Verbum* (1965) all the faithful are encouraged "to acquire by frequent reading of holy scripture, 'the excellent knowledge of Jesus Christ' (Philemon 3: 8)."[64] In *lectio divina*, you read a short passage of scripture and let the Word of God speak to you in your heart. It is a practice which can be done individually or in groups. More information can be found on http://www.eatmyword.com/.

Our Lady

In this book, three specific doctrines or traditions associated with Our Lady are mentioned.

The doctrine of the Immaculate Conception Before all time, the person of Mary, the new Eve, was prepared to be the recipient and the carrier of Jesus. There has always been a tradition in the Church that she must have had a particular grace to merit this honour. In 1854, four years before the apparitions, Pope Pius IX issued an authoritative decree confirming this ancient Church teaching, stating that Mary was immaculately conceived. This means that, through grace won for her by her son Jesus Christ, she was created entirely free from sin – the only person in the human race who has ever been granted this privilege of being born without the stain of the original sin of Adam and Eve. The feast day of the Immaculate Conception is 8 December, nine months before Our Lady's birthday is celebrated on 8 September. Pope Pius IX's successor, Pius XI, chose to canonise Bernadette on 8 December 1933.

Our Lady of Mount Carmel Since the fifteenth century, there has been a popular devotion to Our Lady of Mount Carmel associated with promises of Mary's help for the salvation of the devoted wearer of a dedicated scapular. Mary is said to have given the first scapular to an early Carmelite named St Simon Stock. The final apparition at Lourdes took place on 16 July, the feast of Our Lady of Mount Carmel.

Coronation of Our Lady Bernadette's description of Mary as never looking more beautiful than she did that day, reflects the many images of Mary being crowned in heaven by Jesus. The Crowned Statue of Our Lady, which sits opposite the main basilica and forms the meeting-point and hub of many pilgrimage activities, is one of the most beautiful and memorable in Lourdes. In many Catholic countries, there is a tradition of crowning the Virgin each summer. Our Lady is raised up on high by Jesus, and she in turn points everyone in the direction of her son, just as we see in the Lourdes statue.

Bernadette's prayer from The Dedication to the Queen of Heaven

How happy my heart was, good mother, when I had the happiness to contemplate you!
How I love to remember those sweet moments passed under your gaze full of goodness and mercy for us!
Yes, tender mother, you humbled yourself coming to earth to appear to a feeble child and communicate certain things despite her great unworthiness.
What a great example of humility.
You, the Queen of Heaven and of earth wanted to use the weakest in the earth's eyes.
O Mary, give to the one who dares call herself your child this precious gift of humility.
Help, O tender Mother, your child to imitate you in all and for all, in one word, let me be a child after your heart and that of your dear Son.
You know that my happiness would be to consecrate myself to the religious life, in order to be able to serve you better and your dear Son.
I put all my intentions under your holy protection and beg you to remove all the obstacles if there should be any, because you can better than anyone else.

-St Bernadette, 12 May 1866 (just before leaving Lourdes to go to St Gildard's convent in Nevers)

My soul was glad

A version of Bernadette's prayer that can be sung to the tune *Finlandia*.

My soul was glad, enraptured in your gaze;
O, Queen of Heav'n you set my heart ablaze.
In sweet embrace, so full of saving love
A feeble child was gifted from above.
You came to earth appearing as a sign
Of loving grace, humility divine.

O, Mary help your weakest daughter be
Like you in all for all eternity,
Child of your heart and of your dearest Son
My happiness lies in your love alone
In service true and holy consecration,
I dedicate my love and life to you.

Words: Adam Simon;
Music: Jean Sibelius

References

Bibliography

ESB   A. RAVIER, *Écrits de Sainte Bernadette*, Paris, Lethielleux, 1961.

L   L.M. CROS & M. OLPHE-GALLIARD, *Lourdes 1858 – Témoins de l'Evénement*, Paris, Lethielleux, 1957.

LDA   R. LAURENTIN (in collaboration with B. Billet), *Documents authentiques*, 7 volumes, Paris, Lethielleux, 1957–66.

LHA   R. LAURENTIN, *Histoire authentique des apparitions*, 6 volumes, Paris, Lethielleux, 1961–64.

NDL   H LASSERRE, *Notre Dame de Lourdes*, Paris, Editions DFT, 2003.

R   R. LAURENTIN, *Récit authentique des apparitions* (abbreviated version of LHA), Paris, Lethielleux, 1966.

Communities

Taizé https://www.taize.fr/en

Emmanuel http://www.emmanuelcommunity.co.uk/

The Beatitudes http://beatitudes.org/en/

Chemin Neuf https://www.chemin-neuf.org.uk/en/

Focolare http://www.focolare.org/gb/

L'Arche http://www.larche.org.uk/

Neocatechumenate
http://www.camminoneocatecumenale.it/new/default.asp?lang=en

Apps/Websites

Universalis http://universalis.com/

Pray as you go https://www.pray-as-you-go.org/home/

Notes

1 *Fides et Ratio*, paragraph 1, Pope St John Paul II, 1998

2 LHA 2 p.83

3 LHA 3 p. 152

4 ESB p. 53

5 ESB p. 95

6 R p. 46

7 R p.51

8 R p. 48

9 L p. 36

10 ESB p. 91

11 LHA 2 p. 364

12 LHA 2 p. 328

13 *Lourdes: les Mots de Marie*, Régis-Marie de la Teysonnière, Editions CLD, 2008. This book contains a very full and helpful explanation of the ten phrases uttered by Mary.

14 R p. 69

15 R p. 71

16 *Some of Bernadette's Sayings*, St Gildard's Convent, Nevers

17 LHA 4 p.30

18 LHA 4 p.32

19 LDA 3 p. 73

20 LHA 4 p. 42

21 R p. 77

22 LHA 4 p. 42

23 R p. 102

24 NDL p. 84

25 R p. 108

26 R p. 109

27 R p. 107

28 R p. 117

29 R p. 118

30 R p. 128

31 L p. 162

32 R p. 126

[33] LDA 1 p. 200

[34] LDA 1 p. 200

[35] R p. 145

[36] LDA 1 p. 201

[37] LDA 1 p. 200

[38] *My song is love unknown*, Samuel Crossman

[39] L p. 273

[40] *Fides et Ratio*, 1, Pope St John Paul II, 1998

[41] ESB p. 99

[42] LHA 5 p. 74

[43] R p. 153

[44] LDA 1 p. 175

[45] R p. 173

[46] LHA 5 p. 100

[47] LHA 5 p 203

[48] LHA 5 p. 208

[49] LDA 1 p. 272

[50] LHA 5 p. 201

[51] ESB p. 83

[52] LDA 1 p 205

[53] LDA 1 p 208

[54] LHA 5 p 272

[55] LHA 5 p 275

[56] R p. 225

[57] LHA 6 p 46

[58] *Lumen Gentium* paragraph 11, Constitution of the Church, 1964

[59] LHA 6 p. 159

[60] LDA 6 p 145

[61] *Bernadette Soubirous*, J Barbet, Pau, 1909

[62] R p. 247

[63] *Notre Dame de Lourdes*, Pierre-Rémi Sempé and Jean-Marie Duboë

[64] *Dei Verbum*, Chapter VI, Blessed Pope Paul VI, 1965